THE TRAUMA
OF THE CROSS

*How the Followers of Jesus
Came to Understand
the Crucifixion*

Damian Barry Smyth

PAULIST PRESS
New York / Mahwah, N.J.

Scriptural quotations are from the New Revised Standard Version.

Grateful acknowledgment is made to the following: Excerpt from the service for Tish'a be-Av reprinted by permission of the Central Conference of American Rabbis; brief excerpts from Aeschylus, *Prometheus Bound,* trans. Grene, from *The Complete Greek Tragedies,* ed. Grene and Lattimore, reprinted by permission of the University of Chicago Press; excerpt from Seamus Heaney, "The Tollund Man," from *Wintering Out,* published by Faber and Faber Ltd.; excerpts from Josephus, *The Jewish Wars,* reprinted by permission of Hendrickson Publishers, Inc., Peabody, Mass.; excerpt from Tacitus reprinted by permission of the publishers and the Loeb Classical Library from Tacitus: *The Annals,* Volume V, translated by John Jackson, Cambridge, Mass.: Harvard University Press, 1937.

Art on p. vi by Frank Sabatté, C.S.P.

Cover design by Lynn Else. Cover illustration by Valerie L. Petro.

Library of Congress Cataloging-in-Publication Data

Smyth, Damian Barry, 1934–
    The trauma of the Cross : how the followers of Jesus came to understand the Crucifixion / Damian Barry Smyth.
        p.   cm.
    Includes bibliographical references.
    ISBN 0-8091-3908-1 (alk. paper)
    1. Jesus Christ—Crucifixion—History of doctrines—Early church, ca. 30-600.
I. Title.
    BT450 S66 1999
    232.96'3–dc21   99-047274

Published by Paulist Press
997 Macarthur Boulevard
Mahwah, New Jersey 07430

www.paulistpress.com

Printed and bound in the
United States of America

CONTENTS

Dedication

To Bob, Don, Mike, Colleen, Rey, Bob, Bill, Pete, Roger, Sharon, Al
Amicis

*Third century anti-Christian graffitto from ruins on the
Palatine Hill in Rome. The writing says
"Alexander adores [his] god."*

PREFACE

REVIEWERS of the more popular works of Catholic theology used to remark that such books could be read with profit "not just by priests and religious, but also by the *educated layman.*" This quaint term reminds me of those mythical characters we meet in law school: *the reasonable man* (Torts); *the prudent investor* (Trusts); and, my favorite, *the fertile octogenarian* (Probate). Whether such idealized types *ever* existed in the flesh is clearly a matter for not-too-serious debate.

The present essay—a lawyerly exercise in cross-examination—has its origin in my attempt to educate myself. For the past nine years I have been meeting with a group of lawyer colleagues at 7:00 A.M. every Thursday morning in the eighteenth-floor conference room of a San Francisco financial district bank. At full strength, the group would number eight reasonable men and two reasonable women. Somebody coined the name AMICUS—Attorneys Meeting in Christ to Understand the Scriptures. We take turns making the presentations. When Holy Week of 1996 came around it was my turn again. They seemed to like it. I hope you do, too.

1. NATIONAL TRAUMA

We here highly resolve that these dead shall not have died in vain—that this nation, under God, shall have a new birth of freedom.[1]

WE are all familiar with the standard "traumas" that can afflict individuals: a death in the family, a divorce, loss of employment.... But there are other traumas that can afflict an entire society. They typically constitute the apocalyptic end of the world "as we have known it." Our old world goes up in flames, flames from which a new common identity nevertheless emerges. A classic example would be the American Civil War. Historians agree that the country that issued from the fires of conflict was very different from its ante-bellum predecessor, and that it has endured essentially unchanged to our own day. We would be relatively at home in the United States of 1870. We would be totally at sea in the United States of 1860. More recent but lesser national traumas would include the Depression and the Vietnam War.

The Great Trauma for the first followers of Jesus was his crucifixion. A people in shock probably went through something similar to the five stages outlined by Kübler-Ross in her classic study, *On Death and Dying*: denial and isolation, anger, bargaining, depression,

3

acceptance. While Peter's denial is remembered as the triple denial that he knew Jesus, the denial that provoked the anger of Jesus came earlier in the story:

From that time Jesus began to show his disciples that he must go to Jerusalem and suffer many things from the leaders and chief priests and scribes, and be killed, and on the third day be raised; And Peter took him and began to rebuke him, saying, "God forbid, Lord! This shall never happen to you." (Mt 16:21–22)

This early denial was to have a long life in gnostic circles. Thus in the first half of the second century, Basilides of Alexandria apparently taught that Jesus did not die on the cross. That was really Simon of Cyrene with whom Jesus had switched places! The apocryphal *Acts of John* are equally adamant:

...he showed me a cross of light firmly fixed....This cross then is that which has united all things by the word....But this is not that wooden cross which you shall see when you go down from here; nor am I the man who is on the cross, I whom now you do not see but only hear my voice. I was taken to be what I am not...what they will say of me is mean and unworthy of me....So then I have suffered none of those things which they will say of me....

Similarly in the apocryphal *Gospel of Peter* a crucified Christ suffers no pain and does not really die, but is "taken up" from the cross. The *Gospel of Thomas* has no passion narrative at all. No reference to the passion is to be found in the fragments that remain of the *Gospel of the Hebrews*, the *Gospel of the Ebionites*, or the *Secret Gospel of Mark*.

To others, this reductionist and dismissive gnostic attitude toward the crucifixion was anathema:

In particular, against the docetism of Gnosticism, which accepted Christ as a redemptive hypostasis, to which it applied various Christologies, mostly docetic in character, the Great Church affirmed the doctrine of the incarnation, the integrity of the human nature of Jesus and the salvific character of the crucifixion. (Haardt, 1968)

Thus, for the "Great Church," gnostic denial of the reality of the crucifixion necessarily meant docetic denial of the reality of the incarnation. The "greatness" of this church may be more apparent in retrospect than it was at the time. On the one hand, in those first two preconciliar centuries there seems to have been a bewildering variety of articulations of the mystery of Christ. Those attempted by even such theologians as Tertullian and Origen will not survive post-Nicene scrutiny. Early christology is clearly a work in progress. On the other hand, the 1947 discovery of a rich collection of gnostic materials at Nag Hammadi in Egypt has only reinforced the suspicion occasioned by long-standing disputes between the foremost scholars: what we call "Gnosticism" is not easily reduced to a system. That Gnosticism was widespread is clear from the evidence spread across Samaria, Syria, Asia Minor, Egypt, Italy and North Africa, making it coextensive with the spread of early Christianity. That it was durable is attested to by the presence of such a variety of articulations, those of Valentinians in fourth-century Egypt, of Marcionites in fifth-century Syria and indeed of Mandaeanites in contemporary Iraq. That it was intellectually seductive is attested to by the quality of such adherents as the young Augustine.

The philosophical bedrock of *gnosis* was the dualism that opposes spirit and matter, where matter is inherently evil. The history of this pervasive idea would take us back to ancient Babylonian mythology, and hence through ancient Egypt, Persia and Greece where Plato was its best-known popularizer. In such a scheme, God is pure spirit and cannot be united to matter, which is intrinsically evil. Applied strictly to Christ, for many Gnostics this excluded any material incarnation. Jesus had only an apparent body (*dokeo*, seem or appear, hence "docetism"). Others hesitated to go quite that far, but drew the line at any suffering, especially his sufferings on the cross.

There was another feature of Gnosticism, the importance of which will be more apparent as we develop our theme in later chapters. The dualistic incompatibility of spirit and matter meant that the god of the Gnostics was not to be confused with the creator-god of the early chapters of Genesis. In the gnostic cosmology, the latter was demoted to the subordinate office of demiurge—more or less evil, ignorant, and hostile to God, or at best a degenerate being trying to find his way back to the light. This rejection of the God of the Hebrews made inevitable that rejection of the Hebrew Bible typified by the second-century Gnostic Marcion. Marcion's New Testament was an expurgated collection, containing only Luke and ten Pauline letters in a version purged of Jewish traits—the *reductio ad absurdum* of an anti-Semitic Christianity. As a wealthy ship-owner and as a member of the Christian community in Rome, Marcion was ideally placed to launch the authorized version. Since, however (as we shall see below), the traditional passion narratives are to a phenomenal extent recycled Old Testament, Marcion's dejudaized New Testament was all too consistent with the gnostic agenda and just the thing to provoke his expulsion from the community at Rome and ensure the eventual canonization of a broader collection of sacred books in the "Great Church." Indeed, the delayed reception of the fourth gospel in orthodox circles may have been occasioned not just by the obvious fact that the author marched to a different drummer than did the synoptics, but that the beat was congenial to gnostic ears. Throughout the passion narrative one gets the impression that the Johannine Jesus was not just the principal actor, but also the director and producer of his own movie. Not just the Greatest Story ever Told, but the Greatest Show on Earth.

Although Marcion was charged with corrupting the text of scripture in support of his docetic notions, Professor Bart Ehrman suggests that on the opposite side of the debate an anonymous committee of editors was busy *improving* the same texts to better highlight the humanity of Jesus.[2] Although the Johannine passion narrative may have given the proto-orthodox pause,[3] the Jesus of the

Lucan passion narrative is almost equally in command, particularly if the text is purged of certain phrases which, Ehrman argues, are later interpolations.[4] One such *addition* would be the dramatic "And being in agony he began to pray yet more fervently, and his sweat became like drops of blood falling to the ground." Ehrman's resultant emendations lead him to ask: "Does Luke envisage a passionless passion?" Similarly in John's Passion, Ehrman notes the *omission* in some manuscripts, after Jesus' final "I am thirsty," of the claim that Jesus said this "in order to fulfill the Scripture."

At any rate, by substituting a passionless passion for the brutal fact of the crucifixion of Jesus, the Gnostics spared themselves the original trauma of mainline Christianity and placed themselves irredeemably outside it. For in time, a cross-centered Christianity would become the "Great Church," with Gnosticism largely reduced to an erudite footnote.[5]

In this essay we shall explore how traumatized Jesus People who did not remain in such denial worked through their grief, how they grew toward acceptance of the crucifixion. Since Jesus and the bulk of his first followers were Jews, we can expect that the coping mechanism will be a specifically Jewish one. To find out what this means, therefore, we shall first jump forward some forty years after the crucifixion to what we may call the Great Jewish Trauma.

2. THE GREAT JEWISH TRAUMA

*If I forget you, O Jerusalem,
let my right hand wither!*[1]

IN the first century, the great national trauma for the Jewish people was the Roman War of 66–70. The revolt was initially successful, like that of the Hungarians in 1956 against the Soviets, but the freedom fighters would inevitably be crushed by the Soviet tanks, as the Jews were by the Roman legions. For the Jews, defeat culminated in the destruction of Jerusalem and its world-famous temple. In time, Jerusalem would be rebuilt, if without its defensive walls. But the temple was never rebuilt. Its collapse meant the final collapse of Judaism as Jesus and Peter and James and John and Paul and their contemporaries had known it. As trauma, it was comparable to the Holocaust, the Nazi destruction of six million Jews in our own day.[2]

When the post-Roman-war Jews continued to frequent the synagogues where the scriptures were read to the community, they would have been particularly struck by the Book of Jeremiah, where an angry God curses Judah, threatening the destruction of Jerusalem. And indeed, in Jeremiah's day, such destruction had come to pass at the hands of the Babylonians. The first temple built by the legendary King Solomon was destroyed, and the leaders sent into exile in Babylon. In the eyes of the prophet these foreign invaders were merely the unwitting instruments of God's anger, triggered by Judah's own sinfulness.[3] Some seventy years later, the Persians defeated the Babylonians, and a benevolent King Cyrus permitted the Jews to return to Jerusalem and build what came to be known as the second temple. This was the temple that Herod greatly expanded and that Jesus frequented with his followers.[4]

Already in the gospels, we can hear the rumble of Jewish unrest. Jesus himself seems to transcend politics, adroitly handling a loaded question about Roman taxation and indeed counting the detested tax collectors among his friends. But one or two of his disciples are known *sicarii* (freedom fighters or terrorists, depending on one's point of view).[5] An obscure passage about pigs will be the puzzling remainder of some half-forgotten anti-Roman joke.[6] The term *Messiah* is the flashpoint for nationalist longings for the day when the independent kingdom will be restored as in the days of the legendary King David, Israel's once and future king. The Romans had come by invitation, back when some other superpower seemed to pose a greater threat. But the resultant protectorate and puppet kingdom would in time be reduced to a province, the original military advisers swollen to an army of occupation on the Jordan. The Jewish temple police posted to keep an eye on the volatile crowds are backed up by extra contingents of Roman troops on the major feasts. In Acts a turncoat Paul will have to be hustled out of a turbulent Jerusalem with an escort of three hundred regulars.

Around A.D. 75 the Jewish general Josephus, who had commanded the anti-Roman forces in Galilee during the abortive 66–70 war of Jewish independence, published his seven-volume military memoirs—*The Wars of the Jews*. The more precise subtitle was *The History of the Destruction of Jerusalem*. The thirty-five-year-old veteran, stealing a page from Jeremiah, reckons that a major reason for the disaster was divine wrath directed against Israel for her wickedness. For Josephus's generation, the Book of Jeremiah must have acquired a new topicality:

You have not obeyed me....I will make you a horror to all the kingdoms of the earth. And those who transgressed my covenant...shall be handed over to their enemies and to those who seek their lives. Their corpses will become food for the birds of the air and the wild animals of the earth....I am going to command, says the Lord, and will bring [the Babylonians] back to this city; and they will fight against it, and take it, and burn it with fire. The towns of Judah I will make a desolation without inhabitant. (Jer 34:17–22)

Centuries later Josephus describes the destruction of the second temple in parallel *theological* terms:

So Titus retired into the tower of the Antonia, and resolved to storm the temple the next day, early in the morning, with his whole army, and to encamp about the holy house. But, as for that house, *God had for certain long ago doomed it to the fire*; and that fatal day was come, according to the revolution of the ages....[While Titus slept, some Jews attacked the Romans, who chased them back to the temple area.] At which time one of the soldiers, without staying for any orders, and without any concern or dread upon him at so great an undertaking, and being *hurried on by a certain divine fury,* snatched somewhat out of the materials that were on fire, and being lifted up by another soldier, he set fire to a golden window, through which there was a passage to the rooms that were round the holy house, on the north side of it....And now a certain person came running to Titus, and told him of the fire, as he was resting....Whereupon he rose up in great haste and, as he was, ran to the holy house, in order to put a stop to the fire....Then did Caesar...order them to quench the fire. But they did not hear what he said...the fire proceeded on more and more...and thus the holy house burnt down *without Caesar's approbation...it was fate that decreed it so to be.* (*The Wars of the Jews* 6:4:5–8; emphasis added)

Already in the preface to this history, Josephus had exonerated the Romans, laying responsibility for the destruction of city and temple at the door of those Jews who continued to resist, despite the terms offered by Titus:

I shall relate the barbarity of the tyrants toward the people of their own nation, as well as the indulgence of the Romans in sparing foreigners; and how often Titus, out of his desire to preserve the city and the temple, invited the seditious to come to terms of accommodation...as also, *how the temple was burnt, against the consent of Caesar....* (*The Wars of the Jews,* Preface, 11, emphasis added)

Thus for Josephus, and despite appearances, it was not the Romans who destroyed Jerusalem and the temple. It was Jews themselves who were ultimately responsible. And in the Book of Jeremiah, Josephus finds the key to such self-destruction. This may be less than comforting, but at least it makes some theological sense out of the great disaster and provides a traditional mechanism for coping with the great national trauma. In all of this, Josephus was not original.

The apocalyptic *Vision of Baruch* is equally blunt: "Why is it, O Israel...that you are in the land of your enemies? You have forsaken the fountain of wisdom. If you had walked in the way of the Lord, you would be dwelling in peace forever" (3:10–12).

According to the Babylonian Talmud, God himself lamented: "Woe to me for I have destroyed My house, burned My temple and exiled My children" (Berakhot, 3a).

The fire that destroyed the temple would burn into the collective memory of Judaism, as would the later fires of Auschwitz:

> In the presence of eyes
> which witnessed the slaughter,
> which saw the oppression
> the heart could not bear,
> and as witness the heart
> that once taught compassion
> until the days come to pass
> that crushed human feeling.
> I have taken an oath: To remember it all,
> to remember, not once to forget!
> Forget not one thing to the last generation

> when degradation shall cease,
> to the last, to its ending,
> when the rod of instruction
> shall have come to a conclusion.
> An oath: Not in vain passed over
> the night of terror.
> An oath: No morning shall see me at flesh-pots again.
> An oath: Lest from this we learned nothing.[7]

Lessons were indeed learned. Out of the ashes of the temple a new Judaism would emerge, forging a new Jewish identity. Priest and temple would be replaced by rabbi and synagogue. But this reformed synagogue, hitherto open to pagans who had become honorary Jews ("those who feared God," frequenting the synagogue services without submitting to circumcision), would close its doors to suspect elements, especially those increasingly heterodox Jesus People.

3. "CRUX":
A FOUR-LETTER WORD

Cursed is he who hangs on a tree.[1]

THE great Jesus People trauma was the crucifixion of Jesus of Nazareth. Crucifixion was not simply an early form of capital punishment, comparable to our current electric chair, firing squad or lethal injection. It was, by definition, "cruel and unusual punishment":

> Among the torturous penalties noted in the literature of antiquity, crucifixion was particularly heinous. The act itself damaged no vital organs, nor did it result in excessive bleeding. Hence death came slowly, sometimes after several days, through shock or a painful process of asphyxiation as the muscles used in breathing suffered increasing fatigue.[2]

The process could be accelerated by breaking the legs of the crucified. But the punishment did not end with death: "Often, as a further disgrace, the person was denied burial and the body was left on the cross to serve as carrion for the birds or to rot."[3]

13

The first recorded instances of crucifixion are found in Persia, where it was believed that since the earth was sacred, the burial of the body of a notorious criminal would desecrate the ground. The birds above and the dogs below would dispose of the remains. The Roman poet Horace has a cruel crack about slaves "feeding crows on the cross."[4] I recently heard a grizzled Nevada pastor explain to his congregation that where Jesus said "If I be lifted up..."we would say "If I am strung up..."

Among the Romans, the lawyer Cicero characterized it as *crudelissimum taeterrimumque supplicium* ("that most cruel and disgusting penalty"), primarily used to keep the vast slave population in its place, *servitutis extremum summumque supplicium* ("the supreme and greatest penalty for slaves"). Revolt among slaves was common, and sometimes erupted into full-scale wars. The first slave war broke out in Sicily (139–132 B.C.), and was put down with the crucifixion of 450 slaves. But the most famous slave revolt of all was led by Spartacus. When it too was crushed in 71 B.C., Crassus had more than 6,000 slaves crucified along the Via Appia—that much-traveled highway between Rome and Capua.

Jesus was, of course, no slave. But a secondary purpose of crucifixion was the deterrence of sedition, or what later systems call "crimes against the state." Today states with long-standing pretensions to democracy, when they perceive an internal threat to their existence, will "suspend" civil liberties, give the police "special powers," resort to "in-depth interrogation techniques," set up "special tribunals," organize "detention centers," and institute a whole panoply of draconian measures to stamp out the perceived threat. In a word, crucifixion. Hence, the significance of the inscription attached to the cross: "King of the Jews." Whatever the objections of the chief priests, whatever Jesus himself might have believed or said, the Roman procurator saw Jesus as one who was perceived by many (who knew how many?) to embody the hopes of the "restoration of Israel." This is where the danger to the state lay. Crucifixion puts all would-be saviors and their followers on notice that Rome will not tolerate such delusions of independence. Jesus was not the first Jew to be crucified, and would not be the last. As long as this messiah-of-the month nonsense continued, there would be crucifixions. *Quod scripsi, scripsi!* In 63 B.C., the senator Rabirius stood threatened with crucifixion. In his defense, Cicero argues that among free men the word "cross" should be unmentionable:

> How grievous a thing it is to be disgraced by a public court; how grievous to suffer banishment, and yet in the midst of any such disaster we retain some degree of liberty. Even if we are threatened with death, we may die free men. But the executioner, the veiling of the head and the very word "cross" should be far removed not only from the person of a Roman citizen but his thoughts, his eyes and his ears. For it is not the actual occurrence of these things but the very mention of them that is unworthy of a Roman citizen and a free man.[5]

From Plautus we learn that among the slaves themselves the term *crux*, far from being unmentionable, was the ultimate "four-letter" word bandied about with true gallows humor. But while some of their masters—Seneca, Cicero and especially Varro—might publicly deplore this unspeakable barbarity, the majority preferred to tacitly accept crucifixion as a practical necessity, best not mentioned in polite conversation.

Clearly, then, in such a *crux*-culture no greater trauma could have befallen the followers of Jesus than the ignominious manner of his death. Who would embrace such a faith? "Jews demand miraculous signs and Greeks look for wisdom, but we preach Christ crucified: a stumbling block to Jews and an absurdity to Pagans" (1 Cor 1:22–23).

The sheer absurdity of it in pagan eyes is exemplified in a passage from *True Doctrine* written by Celsus around A.D. 170, as reported in the famous rebuttal by Origen:

> Everywhere they speak in their writings of the tree of life and of resurrection of the flesh by the tree—I imagine because their master was nailed to a cross and was a carpenter by trade. So that if he had happened to be thrown off a cliff, or pushed into a pit, or suffocated by strangling, or if he had been a cobbler or stone-mason or blacksmith,

there would have been a cliff of life above the heavens, or a pit of resurrection, or a rope of immortality, or a blessed stone, or an iron
of love, or a holy hide of leather. Would not an old woman who
sings a story to lull a little child to sleep have been ashamed to
whisper such tales as these?[6]

On a cruder level, the taunting continues in an early third-century
graffito from the Palatine Hill. The hill is named from the imperial
palace, whose builders either tore down or incorporated the buildings already on the hill. Among the latter was the *domus Gelotiana*,
converted into a school for the imperial pages. It portrays a man raising his arm in adoration to another man with the head of an ass
nailed on an upright cross, over the roughly scratched inscription:
ALEZAMENOS SEBETE THEON (Alexander adores [his] god). Another graffito found in the same house reads ALEZAMENOS FEDELIS (Alexander the
Faithful). From contemporary inscriptions, it seems that the term
"*fidelis*" has become interchangeable with "*christianus*".[7] Who
was Alexander? One of the pages who did not laugh at the anti-
Christian jokes? One of the teachers who was "different"? We do
not know. But clearly schoolboys then could be as cruel as they can
be today, and woe betide the outsider.

Given the horrible *crux*-culture, and the consequent vulnerability
to the crudest ridicule, it is no surprise that Professor Nardelli's catalog of paleo-Christian funerary paintings and sculptures from in
and around Rome records only one relief of Christ *carrying* the
cross, and not a single crucifixion.[8] Indeed, the earliest surviving
Christian depictions of the crucifixion of Christ are as late as the fifth
century. On an ivory casket now in the British Museum, a beard-
less Jesus seems to hover majestically on the cross. On a door of the
church of Santa Sabina on Rome's Aventine Hill, a bearded Jesus
seems to stand on the ground, his arms extended in the manner of
the *orans*. It is significant that in the preceding century the first
Christian emperor, Constantine, had abolished crucifixion out of
deference to Christian sensibilities. In other words, it was only
when crucifixion and its attendant *crux*-culture had disappeared

that Christian art could develop the nerve to depict it, albeit in somewhat sanitized forms. As late as the eighth century, in a fresco at
Rome's Santa Maria Antiqua, the crucified Jesus is fully clothed.
While the shame of Jesus' crucifixion was too public to ignore, the
shame of Jesus' burial is quite another question, and one that has
been reexplored only recently. A sporadic trail of articles going back
to the beginning of the century has culminated in speculation by serious scholars that, consistent with his death as a criminal, the body of
Jesus might have been disposed of in shame and dishonor. While
Dominic Crossan has concluded that no one really knows what
became of the body, Raymond E. Brown thinks a criminal's grave the
most likely resting place. This literature has recently been surveyed by
Byron R. McCane, whose review of the gospel accounts against the
background of contemporary Jewish burial practices suggests a
sobering alternative to traditional Easter iconography.[9]

For the Jews of early Roman Palestine, honorable burial was a
cornerstone of family values: the dead were customarily laid to rest
with—or near—their closest relatives. The body was washed with per-
fumes and oils, and bound up with strips of cloth. Burial took place
as soon as possible, often on the day of death. The corpse was placed
in a bier or in a coffin and carried out of town in procession from the
family home to the family tomb—generally a small cave cut from rock
and entered through a narrow opening that could be covered with a
stone. Such rapid entombment has one obvious disadvantage.

> One may go out to the cemetery for three days to inspect the dead
> for a sign of life, without fear that this smacks of heathen practice.
> For it happened that a man was inspected after three days, and he
> went on to live twenty-five years; still another went on to have five
> children and died later.[10]

A week of intense grieving ensued. The relatives of the deceased
stayed home from work, heads covered, receiving condolences. For
the first three days they could leave home only to visit the tomb, to
grieve but also to verify that their loved one was really dead. This first

week was followed by a month of mitigated mourning—the mourners could not leave town, cut their hair or join social gatherings. When that month ended, normal life resumed, except that the mourner's blessing was recited on each visit to the synagogue until a year had passed.

The period of mourning was brought to a close at the end of a year with the rite of *secondary* burial. By now, the flesh had rotted away, and the bones were extracted and placed in an ossuary—a small stone chest. The ossuary was then placed in a niche in the tomb, the final resting place.

Alongside these detailed rituals of honorable burial were the prescriptions for the dishonorable burial of those executed as criminals. Of such the Mishnah records: "They used not to bury him in the burying place of his fathers, but two burying places were kept in readiness by the court, one for them that were beheaded or strangled, and one for them that were stoned or burnt."[11] Since the execution of the criminal was seen as no loss to society, the usual external manifestations of mourning were prohibited. According to the Babylonian Talmud, however, decay of the flesh served to atone for sin. Consequently, after a year the bones could be removed to the family tomb by way of secondary burial. This customary concession serves to explain how archaeologists found the bones of one Yehohanan, the crucified man from Givat ha-Mivtar—complete with the nail which had pierced his ankle—in his family tomb in an ossuary.

When we turn from this archaeological and literary evidence to the New Testament accounts of the burial of Jesus, a certain agenda becomes apparent. For one thing, the hundred pounds of ointment Nicodemus brings to the tomb (Jn 19:39) is grossly excessive, already suggesting a tendency to embellish the facts.

Paul tells the congregation in the synagogue in Pisidian Antioch that "those who live in Jerusalem and their rulers...when they had fulfilled all that was written of him, they took him down from the tree, and laid him in a tomb" (Acts 13:27–29). On the face of it this confirms the expectation engendered by our review of first-century Jewish burial customs in Roman Palestine: Jesus, executed in shame, was buried in shame—laid by the authorities in the common tomb for criminals without any public rites of mourning. The latter lacuna is accentuated by gospel specifics of mourning surrounding other deaths: the funeral of the daughter of Jairus; Mary and Martha mourning Lazarus; the son who cannot follow Jesus because he is still mourning his father's death.

Still consistent with this reading, the later Mark has the body of Jesus wrapped in linen and sealed in a tomb by Joseph of Arimathea, *a member of the council.* Yet later retellings have Joseph dissenting from his colleagues' decision (Luke), and evolving into a secret disciple of Jesus (Matthew, John), who asks for the body of Jesus *before* the crucifixion *(Gos. Pet.).* Indeed, the *Gospel of Peter* has Jesus buried in the tomb of a wealthy and powerful family, and his death is properly mourned. This expunges the last vestiges of shame from the account of the burial of Jesus. The shame of the crucifixion, however, would not be so easily airbrushed out.

4. THE EMMAUS CURE

Memory does not simply happen; it is always motivated, always mediated, by complex mechanisms.[1]

THE earliest Christian "historian," Luke, describes the response of the first Jesus People to his crucifixion in the final chapter of his first volume:

> Now on the same day [the first day of the week following the crucifixion] two of them were going to a village called Emmaus, about seven miles from Jerusalem, and talking with each other about all these things that had happened. While they were talking and discussing, Jesus himself came near and went with them, but their eyes were kept from recognizing him. And he said to them, "What are you discussing with each other while you walk along?" They stood still, looking sad. Then one of them, whose name was Cleopas, answered him, "Are you the only stranger in Jerusalem, who does not know the things that have taken place there in these days?" He asked them, "What things?" They replied, "The things about Jesus of Nazareth, who was a prophet mighty in deed and word before God and all the people, and how our chief priests and leaders handed him over to be condemned to death and crucified him. But we had hopes that he was the one to redeem Israel...."

20

Then he said to them, "Oh, how foolish you are, and how slow of heart to believe all that the prophets have declared! Was it not necessary that the Messiah should suffer these things and then enter into his glory?" Then beginning with Moses and all the prophets, he interpreted to them the things about himself in all the scriptures. [Breaking of the bread] "Were not our hearts burning within us while he was talking to us on the way, while he was opening the scriptures to us?" [Return to Jerusalem, where they are told that the Lord has risen indeed, and has appeared to Simon.] Then they told what had happened on the way, and how he had been made known to them in the breaking of the bread.

I wonder if Luke has here telescoped into the experience of a single couple on a single day that of the general crowd of Jesus People in the months and years following the crucifixion.[2] Let us examine the individual elements:–

- Some scholars, such as Murphy-O'Connor, see the two as Cleophas and his wife. Are they thus prototypes of all the men *and women* (Luke is recognizably proto-feminist) who first followed Jesus?
- The first reaction of these disciples to the Great Trauma is flight—anywhere but Jerusalem, with its unbearable memories.
- Like all the traumatized, they are obsessed; their sole and perpetual topic of conversation is the crucifixion: "...talking with each other about all these things...while they were talking and discussing...what are you discussing?" They cannot understand why everybody else does not share their obsession: "Are you the only stranger in Jerusalem who does not know...?"
- They enunciate the essence of the Great Trauma: Jesus, clearly a prophet, was handed over by their own chief priests and leaders to be crucified, the very one they *had* hoped would redeem Israel. Their hope died with Jesus.
- Early stories, *women's* stories, of an empty tomb only compounded the confusion. This is important: the traumatized Jesus

People do not equate the empty tomb with resurrection. It simply adds to the grief. We do not even have his tomb to visit!

- The answer of the "stranger" is not to point to himself, but to the scriptures: "Beginning with Moses and all the prophets, he interpreted to them the things about himself in *all the scriptures.*" It seems improbable that such a vast survey of virtually the whole of scripture could be expounded, much less *absorbed*, in a few hours, and by people in a state of shock.
- Luke's account does emphasize that the revelation/recognition of the risen Jesus is anything but instantaneous. It will not be complete until that long day has drawn to its close.
- First, the fire that Jesus had originally kindled in their hearts, and which the Great Trauma had extinguished, must be relit. This is accomplished through a rereading of the scriptures, now read as never before. This Jesus-illuminated reading of the whole of the Jewish scriptures is done "in the Way." This term, "the Way" was Lucan shorthand for the new way of life inspired by Jesus. See Acts 9:1–2: "Meanwhile Saul, still breathing threats and murder against the disciples of the Lord, went to the high priest and asked him for letters to the synagogues at Damascus, so that if he found *any who belonged to the Way,* men and women, he might bring them bound to Jerusalem." "The subtle, yet highly deliberate, use of this Lucan motif is not to be missed."[3]
- When the light finally dawns, it is in that most grace-filled moment: *the breaking of the bread.* Early in his second volume, Luke will see this as an essential feature of the Way: "They [the 3,000 newly baptized] devoted themselves to the apostles' teaching and fellowship, to *the breaking of bread* and the prayers" (Acts 2:42). Luke's mentor on the Way, Paul, assumes the central role of this community meal: "The *bread that we break,* is it not a sharing in the body of Christ?" (1 Cor 10:16)
- The Emmaus experience is corroborated by the account of the appearance to Simon. But the faith of the community, sought

in the pages of the scriptures (at first laboriously, but then with growing conviction), unexpectedly found in the breaking of bread, does not derive from the apparition to Simon. This rather serves to confirm Simon's authority in the community, an authority consolidated in those first chapters of Luke's second volume, which could be subtitled Acts of Peter. The primary source of resurrection faith for the community is to be sought in the Jesus-led searching of the scriptures culminating in the epiphanic breaking of bread. The body of Jesus, not to be found in a tomb, yields place to the body of Christ nourished by the rereading of the scriptures and the breaking of the bread.

5. SEARCHING THE SCRIPTURES

Like one from whom men hide their faces he was despised, and we esteemed him not.[1]

IF the Emmaus experience described by Luke involved the whole crowd (not yet a *community*) of Jesus People, and was a process lasting for an extended period of time, let us see if we can visualize some steps in this process. The first Jesus People continued to frequent their synagogues, where they listened to the cycle of readings "beginning with Moses and all the prophets." As they listened to these passages familiar since childhood, something odd began to occur. Obsessed with the death of Jesus, they began to see unexpected connections. The old familiar scriptures began to resonate in their new Jesus consciousness in an entirely new way.

As we explore this process in detail, we will be struck by what appears to be a cavalier attitude to certain principles of textual interpretation that any lawyer, any historian, any scholar would consider inviolable. We require that a text be interpreted in its context. We ask, what was the intent of the original author. We will find our proto-Christian writers blissfully unhampered by such pedestrian considerations. As one commentator puts it: "The New Testament begins...not with the original meaning of Old Testament texts, but with the facts of Jesus' life, and then it finds in the Old Testament an explanation of these attested facts."[2] As the same commentator points out, this to us academically indefensible method was inherited from contemporary Judaism: "Both the Qumran hermeneutics and the rabbinical hermeneutics are supremely oblivious to contextual exegesis whenever they wish."[3] If this sounds uncomfortably like the freewheeling, self-serving free association of the televangelist for the more fastidious among us, we just have to swallow hard and accept the massively documented phenomenon.

And so our proto-Christians might naturally ask: If Jesus was the Son of God, how could his Father abandon him to such a death? In Genesis, the well-known story of the sacrifice of Isaac would suggest an answer. In his love for us, *God did not spare his own son.* Before the passion narratives as we know them were written down, ex-Pharisee Saul/Paul would echo this early discovery in his letter to the Romans.[4]

Again, one might well ask: How could Jesus be sold by one of his own? The Genesis story of Joseph recounts his being sold into Egypt for *twenty pieces of silver by his own brothers*—a betrayal that would paradoxically lead to their eventual salvation by the same magnanimous Joseph. This apparently unforgivable act was all part of God's long-term plan. As Joseph, now ascended to almighty Pharaoh's right hand, reassures his frightened brothers: "God sent me before you to preserve for you a remnant on earth, and to keep alive for you many survivors. So it was not you who sent me here, but God...."

The equally novelistic Second Book of Samuel, chapters 15 and 16, provides further detail. King David, betrayed by his most trusted friend Ahithophel, crossed the Wadi Kidron and went to the Mount of Olives where he wept and prayed—an agony in the garden. David, anxious that his faithful followers should not share his fate, then sent them back to Jerusalem to wait for better days. Ahithophel counsels the usurping Absalom about how to eliminate David. His advice is opposed by another counselor, Hushai, who has been planted in Absalom's court by David for that very purpose.

To Ahitophel's mortification, "Absalom and all the men of Israel said: The counsel of Hushai the Archite is better than the counsel of Ahithophel." This was more than he could bear. The Bible goes on to describe his end. "When Ahithophel saw that his counsel was not followed, he saddled his donkey and went off home to his own city. He set his house in order, and hanged himself; he died and was buried in the tomb of his father." Jesus is hailed in the gospels as "Son of David," where he follows the above Davidic pattern in his final hours. The Synoptics have Jesus heading from the Last Supper (where his betrayer is identified as *one of his twelve closest followers*) to the *Mount of Olives*. The fourth gospel does not parrot this identification, but is equivalently evocative of 2 Samuel in sending Jesus/David *across the Kidron valley*. Judas, like Ahithophel, finds his final overtures to the council scornfully rejected. "*He departed*; and *he went and hanged himself*," reports Matthew. Matthew elaborates further on the death of Judas, showing him throwing the thirty pieces of silver in the sanctuary—leaving the priests to apply this otherwise unusable "blood money" to the purchase of a potter's field as a graveyard for foreigners. This is Matthew's cue for another of his fulfillment texts:

> The word spoken through the prophet Jeremiah was then fulfilled: And they took the thirty silver pieces, the sum at which the precious One was priced by the children of Israel, and they gave them for the potter's field, just as the Lord directed me.

Luke's etiology ("How did that field just outside town get such a bad name?") is somewhat different. In the first chapter of Acts, it is Judas himself who buys the field with his ill-gotten gains. Then, presumably when out inspecting his acquisition. "He fell headlong, and burst open, and all his entrails poured out. Everybody in Jerusalem heard about it, and the plot came to be called 'Bloody Acre,' in their language Hakeldama."

Unlike Matthew, Luke is not really interested in "searching the scriptures" for the meaning of this demise. Luke's focus is on the restoration of the integrity of the Twelve by the (divine) election of

Matthias, in fulfillment therefore of other passages from scripture: "*Let his homestead become desolate, and let there be no one to live in it*" (Ps 69:25); and again, "*Let someone else take over his office*" (Ps 109:8).

Thus, the same New Testament event—the death of Judas—is recounted differently, depending on the narrator's focus.[5] Each of the resultant versions are linked to entirely different Old Testament texts. This is not to suggest that Judas's end is pure fiction. It is rather to suggest that the common tradition is refracted through the prism of each narrator's unique theological agenda, bolstered by the selection of different fulfillment texts.

Why did Jesus meet such a bloody end? Exodus describes how the blood of the Passover lamb was the salvation of the people of God:

> Then Moses called all the elders of Israel and said to them, "Go, select lambs for your families, and slaughter the passover lamb. Take a bunch of hyssop, dip it in the blood that is in the basin, and touch the lintel and the two doorposts with the blood in the basin. None of you shall go outside the door of your house until morning. For the Lord will pass through to strike down the Egyptians; when he sees the blood on the lintel and on the two doorposts the Lord will pass over that door and will not allow the destroyer to enter your houses to strike you down. You shall observe this rite as a perpetual ordinance for you and your children....And when your children ask you, 'What do you mean by this observance?' you shall say, 'It is the passover sacrifice to the Lord, for he passed over the house of the Israelites in Egypt, when he struck down the Egyptians but spared our houses.'"

Thanks to an annual ritual retelling and reenactment, this episode of the passover lamb becomes the kernel of the founding myth, and the heart of a "birthday" celebration for the whole people of Israel. It was unthinkable for Jewish followers of the Jew Jesus to jettison Passover, the greatest feast in their calendar. In this context, Jesus is perceived as the *lamb of God*, and a transformed Passover becomes Easter—the greatest feast in the old calendar begets the greatest feast in a new calendar.

What could possibly be the point of the terrible sufferings of Jesus? The Suffering Servant passages in Isaiah reverberate throughout the passion narrative, and for centuries have provided a plaintive backdrop to our Good Friday liturgies. One example reads, or rather sings:

> He had no beauty or majesty to attract us to him,
>   nothing in his appearance that we should desire him.
> He was despised and rejected by men,
>   a man of sorrows, and familiar with suffering.
> Like one from whom men hide their faces
>   he was despised, and we esteemed him not.
> Surely he took up our infirmities
>   and carried our sorrows,
> yet we considered him stricken by God,
>   smitten by him, and afflicted.
> But he was pierced for our transgressions,
>   he was crushed for our iniquities;
> the punishment that brought us peace was upon him,
>   and by his wounds we are healed.
> We all, like sheep, have gone astray,
>   each of us has turned to his own way;
> and the LORD has laid on him
>   the iniquity of us all.
> He was oppressed and afflicted,
>   yet he did not open his mouth;
> he was led like a lamb to the slaughter,
>   and as a sheep before her shearers is silent,
> so he did not open his mouth.
> By oppression and judgment he was taken away.
> And who can speak of his descendants?
>   For he was cut off from the land of the living;
> for the transgression of my people he was stricken.
>   He was assigned a grave with the wicked,
> and with the rich in his death,
>   though he had done no violence,
> nor was any deceit in his mouth.

Yet it was the LORD's will to crush him and cause him to suffer,
and though the LORD makes his life a guilt offering,
  he will see his offspring and prolong his days,
and the will of the LORD will prosper in his hand.
  After the suffering of his soul,
he will see the light of life and be satisfied;
    by his knowledge my righteous servant will justify many,
and he will bear their iniquities.
  Therefore I will give him a portion among the great,
and he will divide the spoils with the strong,
    because he poured out his life unto death,
and was numbered with the transgressors.
  For he bore the sin of many,
and made intercession for the transgressors.

In Luke's second volume, Acts of the Apostles, an officer of the court of Her Royal Majesty Queen Candace of Ethiopia reads the above passage and is puzzled by the reference to sheep led to the slaughter.[6] "The eunuch asked Philip, 'Tell me, please, who is the prophet talking about, himself or someone else?' Then Philip began with that very passage of Scripture and told him the good news about Jesus."

Scholars argue over how many Isaiah passages are echoed in the passion narratives. This serves to illustrate that the perception of such *implicit* parallels verges on the subjective. All, however, agree that the tone of the narratives is heavily Isaian. There is no mistaking Shakespeare, Beethoven or Isaiah. The poet Robert Pinsky recalls laboriously reciting a Hebrew text from Isaiah as "my first encounter with great poetry."[7] This greatness is identified by Luis Alonso Schökel as classical:

...some special traits permit us to consider Isaiah as a classical writer: classical because of the distance he places between himself and the poem. That is, rather than allowing the experience, however traumatic, to break out spontaneously like a scream, he transforms it consciously into poetry.[8]

It was unthinkable that a poet and prophet of Isaiah's stature should not be a primary target of the proto-Jewish-Christian searching of the scriptures. The Schökel analysis suggests how this same Isaiah was the antidote for this deeply traumatized community. The Lamentations of Jeremiah, with their lyric irruptions, might fill the night. The more measured melody of Isaiah would break in with the morning.

To which one might rightly respond: If Isaiah sings unforgettably of the Suffering Servant, Jeremiah (as we shall see in our next chapter) *was* the Suffering Servant.

6. THE PASSION OF JEREMIAH

*I have become a laughingstock all day long;
everyone mocks me.[1]*

THE story of Jeremiah provides abundant material for proto-Christian reflection. In Jeremiah 18, the Lord sends the prophet to watch the potter at work, shaping and reshaping his pots. The Lord points out that He makes and breaks the nations, and orders Jeremiah to warn Judah and Jerusalem to mend their wicked ways. But this warning is rejected, and the messenger becomes the target of hatred: "Then they said, 'Come, let us make plots against Jeremiah....Come, let us bring charges against him, and let us not heed any of his words'" (Jer 18:18).

The Lord's response is to have Jeremiah buy an earthenware jug from the potter, and take with him "some of the elders of the people and some of the senior priests," to the entry of the Potsherd Gate:

Then you shall break the jug in the sight of those who go with you, and shall say to them: Thus says the Lord of hosts: So will I break this people and this city, as one breaks a potter's vessel, so they shall bury until there is no more room to bury. Thus will I do to this place, says the Lord, and to its inhabitants....(Jer 19:10–12)

31

The reaction from the priest who was the chief of the temple police[2] to the unwelcome message is immediate:

Now the priest Pashtur son of Immer, who was chief officer in the house of the Lord, heard Jeremiah prophesying these things. Then Pashtur struck the prophet Jeremiah, and put him in the stocks that were in the upper Benjamin Gate of the house of the Lord. (Jer 20:1–2)

By now the unfortunate Jeremiah has had more than enough of this, and complains to God:

> I have become a laughingstock all day long;
> everyone mocks me....
> For I hear many whispering
> "Terror is all around!
> Denounce him! Let us denounce him!"
> All my close friends
> are watching for me to stumble.... (Jer 20:7–10)

God simply sends Jeremiah out again with a message directed against the leaders of the people: "Woe to the shepherds who destroy and scatter the sheep of my pasture!" (Jer 23:1). Message after message Jeremiah relays to the priests and leaders, all unwelcome. But the least welcome message of all is that of the impending destruction of Jerusalem and the temple (Jer 26):

Thus says the Lord: Stand in the court of the Lord's house, and speak to all the cities of Judah that come to worship in the house of the Lord; speak to them all the words that I command you; do not hold back a word....If you will not listen to me...then I will make this house like Shiloh, and I will make this city a curse for all the nations of the earth....And when Jeremiah had finished speaking all that the Lord had commanded him to speak to all the people, then the priests and the prophets and all the people laid hold of him, saying: "You shall die!"...When the officials of Judah heard these things, they came up from the king's house to the house of the Lord and took their seat in the entry of the New Gate of the house of the Lord. Then the priests and prophets said to the officials and to all the people: "This man deserves the sentence of death because he has prophesied against this city, as you have heard with your own ears." Then Jeremiah spoke... "Only know for certain that if you put me to death, you will be bringing innocent blood upon yourselves and upon this city and its inhabitants, for in truth the Lord sent me to you to speak all these words in your ears."

Interestingly, "the officials and all the people" acquit Jeremiah, and indeed some of the elders rise to point out a clear precedent where the prophet Micah warned with impunity an earlier king that "Jerusalem will become a heap of ruins."

In Jeremiah 38, the prophet again falls foul of the leaders for preaching sedition:

Shephatiah son of Mattan, Gedaliah son of Pashhur, Jehucal son of Shelemiah, and Pashhur son of Malkijah heard what Jeremiah was telling all the people when he said, "This is what the LORD says: 'Whoever stays in this city will die by the sword, famine or plague, but whoever goes over to the Babylonians will live. He will escape with his life; he will live.' And this is what the LORD says: 'This city will certainly be handed over to the army of the king of Babylon, who will capture it.'" Then the officials said to the king, "This man should be put to death. He is discouraging the soldiers who are left in this city, as well as all the people, by the things he is saying to them. This man is not seeking the good of these people but their ruin." "He is in your hands," King Zedekiah answered. "The king can do nothing to oppose you." So they took Jeremiah and put him into the cistern of Malkijah, the king's son, which was in the courtyard of the guard. They lowered Jeremiah by ropes into the cistern; it had no water in it, only mud, and Jeremiah sank down into the mud. But Ebed-Melech, a Cushite, an official in the royal palace, heard that they had put Jeremiah into the cistern. While the king was sitting in the Benjamin Gate, Ebed-Melech went out of the palace and said to him, "My lord the king, these men have acted wickedly in all they have done to Jeremiah the prophet. They have thrown him into a cistern, where he will starve to death when there is no longer any bread in the city." Then the king commanded Ebed-Melech the Cushite, "Take thirty men from here with you and lift Jeremiah the prophet out of the cistern before he dies." ...And Jeremiah remained in the court-yard of the guard until the day Jerusalem was captured.

Rereading such familiar passages, the first Jesus People would have readily remembered Jesus as a prophet in the pattern of the long-suffering Jeremiah: the confrontation with the religious authorities; the violent sign (the shattering of the jug; the whipping of the temple bankers); the behind-doors plotting against the prophet; the intervention of the temple police; the indignation of the high priest; the mockery by enemies; the abandonment by friends; the prophet's own deep depression and wish to be released from his deadly mission; the reluctant abdication of secular authority under pressure; the death sentence, "bringing innocent blood upon the city and its inhabitants." Thus in the passion of Jeremiah, the first Jesus People had more than just a random selection of "usable" texts; they had a *detailed blue-print* for a passion of Jesus.

Given the wealth of detail in the Jeremiah blueprint, we must not overlook the one detail that all our searching of the Jewish scriptures will not find: Jeremiah is not crucified. For crucifixion, we must wait for the coming of the Romans. And the crucifixion of Jesus is a mat-ter of Roman record. Roman historian Tacitus refers to a certain sect living in the city "*quos...vulgus christianos appellabat*," who were popularly nicknamed "Christians." Since the term "*christianus*" was probably derogatory in origin, acquiring respectability with time (like Quaker,[3] Whig, Tory, Roman Catholic...), perhaps a better translation is "christers."[4] But why this nickname? "Their founder, a certain Christus, had undergone the death penalty in the reign of Tiberius, by sentence of the procurator Pontius Pilate."[5]

The crucifixion is the grain of Roman sand in the Jewish oyster, the alien irritant that leads to the formation of the passion pearl.

7. PSALMS OF SUFFERING AND SOLACE

All who see me mock at me.
They make mouths at me; they shake their heads.[1]

JUST as the first Jesus People continued to listen to the synagogue readings, so they continued to sing the psalms. In a final post mortem apparition to the still-terrified Jesus People, Luke has Jesus issue a final reminder "...that everything written about me in the law of Moses, the prophets *and the psalms* must be fulfilled.[2] Then he opened their minds to understanding the scriptures" (Lk 24:44–45). In fact, the psalms were to prove a fertile source of *secondary* detail, elaborating on what had actually been done to Jesus in the course of his passion.[3]

First, let us see what Luke himself records as the message of the psalms for those traumatized by the crucifixion of Jesus. Luke is the only evangelist to continue the gospel story into a second volume, mapping the continuation of "the Way" from its point of departure in Jerusalem to its point of arrival in Rome, and introducing a copernican shift into the universe of salvation. Given his evident concern with that critical emergence of Christianity from its Jewish matrix into the

Greco-Roman world, he must address Rome's role in the crucifixion. For if Jesus was not only the long-awaited Messiah for the Jews, but one whose message was to be proclaimed to all nations now under Roman rule, how can we explain the unholy and unlikely alliance of Roman and Jew against Jesus? Psalm 2 provides the key:

> Why did the pagans rage
> and the people imagine vain things?
> The kings of the earth took their stand
> and the rulers have gathered together
> against the Lord and against his Messiah.

The pagans are the Romans; the people are the Jews; the king is Herod; the ruler is Pilate—united in their unlikely alliance against the Lord and against the Lord's Anointed *(Christos)*.[4] Unlikely, for Luke in his earlier volume reports: "That same day Herod and Pilate became friends with each other; before this they had been enemies." Luke diplomatically refrains from quoting the rest of the psalm, where God laughs at the puny efforts of earthly authorities to oppose his plans, and which concludes with a warning:

> Now, therefore, O kings, be wise;
> be warned, O rulers of the earth.
> Serve the Lord with fear,
> with trembling, kiss his feet,
> or he will be angry, and you will perish in the way;
> for his wrath is quickly kindled.

Luke's Judeo-Christian readers were too familiar with the thundering conclusion of Psalm 2 to need an express reminder, and for the conciliatory Luke there was simply no point in gratuitous badgering of the authorities. This new reading of an old song is for in-house consumption. Indeed, Luke's report of this "community meditation" on Psalm 2, triggered by the Jewish council's release of Peter and John, concludes with a confirming earthquake whose function is not to intimidate the authorities, but to inspire the disciples to "continue to speak the word of God with boldness"—an in-house earthquake.

While the broader political framework of the crucifixion may have been of particular concern to the well-educated and well-traveled Luke, the ordinary Jesus Person remained hypnotized by the revolting details of the execution itself. For all such mourners what better words to describe the cruel treatment of the Crucified One than those of Psalm 22?:

> O my God, I cry by day, but you do not answer;
> and by night, but find no rest....
> But I am worm and not human;
> scorned by others, and despised by the people.
> All who see me mock at me;
> They make mouths at me, they shake their heads;
> "Commit your cause to the LORD; let him deliver—
> let him rescue the one in whom he delights!"...
> Many bulls encircle me,
> Strong bulls of Bashan surround me;
> They open wide their mouths at me,
> like a ravening and roaring lion...
> For dogs are all around me;
> a company of evildoers encircles me.
> My hands and feet have shriveled;
> I can count all my bones.
> They stare and gloat over me;
> they divide my clothes among themselves,
> and for my clothing, they casts lots.

For those sufficiently familiar with Mark's characteristically unadorned account of the crucifixion, there is a growing sense of *déjà vu* on reading Psalm 22. An immediate echo is found in the opening verse, corresponding to *Eloi, Eloi, lama sabachthani?* Mark underscores the drama of this quotation by leaving it in the original Aramaic, which he then translates: My God, my God, why have you forsaken me? A further echo is sounded by the *casting of lots for the garments.* This makes us pause and sends us back for a second, closer search for other possible parallels. The two bandits, one on his right and one on his left, join in the general taunting, like the hostile *bulls, lions, dogs* surrounding the stricken psalmist; they *wag their heads, reviling* him, for he *cannot save himself.* The only response of the victim is a *great cry* (in Mark, a wordless cry) to which God does not respond. Thus, as we continue to examine Psalm 22 and Mark 15 side by side, we see more and more parallels. The psalm "quotations" in the Marcan account of the crucifixion/mockery/death of Jesus tend to be more implicit than explicit, and scholars may argue over details. Nonetheless, when the entire psalm is reread in the light of the Marcan account, one cannot but be struck by the fact that the imagined echoes are not restricted to the discrete verses identified above in piecemeal fashion. Rather, the entire psalm reads like Mark set to music, while Mark reads like the heart-rending old song condensed to prose. In mining Psalm 22 to depict the sufferings of the crucified one, how could Mark have resisted quoting these other graphic lines?

> I am poured out like water,
> and all my bones are out of joint;
> my heart is like wax;
> it is melted within my breast;
> my mouth is dried up like a potsherd,
> and my tongue sticks to my jaws;
> you lay me in the dust of death.

But Mark's readers knew perfectly well which psalm he was "quoting" and where to find it. Indeed, they probably knew most of the psalms by heart. His cryptic account would more than suffice to open the floodgates. Thus prompted, the Jewish readers of Mark—the earliest of our canonical gospels—would set out eagerly to "search the scriptures" a good decade or two before Luke would so enjoin them. Above all, they would find hope reborn out of darkest tragedy in the unquoted triumphant conclusion of Psalm 22, which turns the corner proclaiming:

> For he did not despise or abhor
> the affliction of the afflicted;
> he did not hide his face from me,
> but heard when I cried to him.

Matthew corrects Mark's Aramaic to read *Eli, Eli*....Luke, toning down the more distressing elements, omits this shattering cry. Nor is it found in John's account, where a majestic Jesus proceeds through his passion as if starring in and directing his own movie. Each evangelist leaves his theological fingerprints all over the passion narrative.

Psalm 34 sings of a God who keeps all the bones of the righteous: "not one of them will be broken." This sign of divine protection may be linked with another text which prescribes that the bones of the passover lamb are not to be broken, to be mulled over and emerge decades later in the passion narrative of the fourth gospel:

> Then the soldiers came and broke the legs of the first and of the other who had been crucified with him. But when they came to Jesus and saw that he was already dead, they did not break his legs....These things occurred so that the scripture might be fulfilled: "None of his bones shall be broken."

The trusted friend of Psalm 41 who shared the just man's bread only to raise up his heel against him is readily recognized and in due course makes his appearance in the fourth gospel, where the imminent betrayal by Judas casts a dark shadow over the joy of the Last Supper:

> "I am not referring to all of you; I know those I have chosen. But this is to fulfill the scripture: *He who shares my bread has lifted up his heel against me.* I am telling you now before it happens, so that when it does happen you will believe that I am He...." After he had said this, Jesus was troubled in spirit and testified, "I tell you the truth, one of you is going to betray me."

This selective survey of passages from the psalms which find their way into the earliest reflections on the meaning of the crucifixion does not pretend to be exhaustive, any more than the prior chapters' survey of similarly utilized texts from the Law and the Prophets. A systematic listing of all such likely texts is set forth in Appendix VII of Raymond Brown's *The Death of the Messiah.* As one spends time with the Bible, one's ears gradually become attuned to the realization that the whole of it, Old and New Testaments, forms one vast echo chamber.

8. THE CHRISTIAN FAMILY QUILT

When life goes to pieces, try quilting.

WE have explored above a selective sampling of passages from all across the scriptures which the first Jesus People reworked to articulate a theology of the cross. It thus appears that a variety of events, historically distinct, recorded by different writers at different times, interact within the reading community to reveal common patterns and eventually fuse "all of the above," into a denser multilayered deposit after the pattern of the passion of Jeremiah.

A feature in the *New York Times* (4/4/96) on the current revival of quilting among black women suggests an interesting parallel:

> Oral tradition and the world of the quilt constitute the most important record we have of black families....It has historically provided women an opportunity to come together to work, exchange ideas and share in each others troubles....In times of social fragmentation it offers an antidote, common ground. In many ways...quilting is a healing art. Today, in anonymous urban settings...the quilters make a connection, as if through sewing they stitch themselves with one another....Collectively, these quilters are redefining tradition....When life goes to pieces, try quilting.

41

When life as they had known it went to pieces, the first Jesus People came together to work ("I'm going fishing," said Peter), to exchange ideas, and to share their common trouble. As they continued to read the Jewish scriptures certain pages seemed to detach themselves from the original context. As more and more pages did this for different readers, and as they excitedly shared their findings, they began to stitch these well-worn texts together into patchwork quilts that would become precious Christian family heirlooms.

While the materials were traditional Jewish, the emerging design was something altogether new, for these Jewish Jesus People were "redefining tradition." And as they "sewed," they stitched themselves together into a new community. As the years passed, the quilts grew in number. In time, certain examples would emerge as the most popular "patterns," and would be incorporated into the more ambitious community projects that came to be ascribed to "Mark," "Matthew," "Luke," and "John."[1]

It seems a fair assumption that this proto-Christian "quilting bee" took on a liturgical format, evolving into a standardized service combining selected old Jewish scripture readings and new Christian hymns and prayers to commemorate the passion/death/resurrection of Jesus Christ—an early and weekly model that will evolve into our annual Easter Triduum.

From the very beginning this took place on "the first day of the week," that is, on the weekly memorial of the day Christ was raised from the dead.[2]

> On the evening of that first day of the week, when the disciples were together, with the doors locked for fear of the Jews, Jesus came and stood among them and said, "Peace be with you!" After he said this, he showed them his hands and side. The disciples were overjoyed when they saw the Lord. (Jn 20:19–20)

A similar appearance, even more dramatic, is made on the first day of the following week:

A week later his disciples were in the house again, and Thomas was with them. Though the doors were locked, Jesus came and stood among them and said, "Peace be with you!" Then he said to Thomas, "Put your finger here; see my hands. Reach out your hand and put it into my side. Stop doubting and believe." Thomas said to him, "My Lord and my God!" (Jn 20:26–28)

These accounts underline a basic theme. The risen Christ identifies himself by showing his wounds, thus planting the cross firmly in the soil of the early communities. The faith demanded of all "doubting Thomases" (and there were many such in those early days) required no less.

The Acts of the Apostles records one such weekly meeting at Troas, with Paul presiding. It takes place during the night of the first day of the week. Since the Jewish day, then as now, went from evening to evening, this means Saturday night into Sunday morning. The faithful meet in an upper room at the home of one of the group. There are no church buildings yet. The church is a church of "living stones." Paul preaches at some length, presumably on the scriptures. As at Emmaus, the communal searching of the scriptures under apostolic guidance climaxes in the breaking of the bread. This is the central and climactic element that has already come to designate the weekly meeting: "On the first day of the week, when *we met to break bread*...." The meeting concludes at dawn.

Christians do not have to be liturgical historians to recognize this early pattern. The weekly gathering at Troas was memorable, however, not merely because of the visiting preacher. Paul, about to sail away that Sunday, prolonged his preaching well into the night. Young Eutychus, who was sitting "in the window," began to sink into a deep sleep. The window was evidently open, and Eutychus fell to the ground three floors below. He was, the text laconically reports, "picked up dead." Paul, however, went down, took Eutychus up in his arms, and announced: "Do not be alarmed, for his life is in him." In this context the "Do not be alarmed" seems to echo the "Fear not" of the risen Christ, and young Eutychus seems, dramatically if unwittingly, to reenact in his person that very mystery of death and resurrection that the community gathers to reenact ritually in the breaking of bread.

While such texts illustrate the format taken by those proto-Christian quilting bees, our focus in the present study is on the materials used—those scraps of Hebrew prophecy, those snatches of psalms. The author of Acts does not tell us which were popular in that upper room in Troas. But then he scarcely needs to. For there are few things more conservative (in the very best sense) than liturgy. The songs that Israel sang by the waters of Babylon are sung in the synagogue today, and Hebrew class for children ensures that all can join in.

In our Christian liturgy it is in Holy Week that, as you might expect, that resistance to change is most evident. Phrases in now forgotten languages linger on. Few know anything about, much less of, Aramaic. But the last words of Jesus on the cross are sacrosanct: *Eli, Eli, lama sabacthani*. Greek, the language of the early Christian hymns, lingers on: *Hagios, O Theos*. In the darkness of the night, the monastic vigil resonates to the Lamentations of Jeremiah, where desolation is kept in check by a discipline which insists that each verse shall begin with the next letter of the Hebrew alphabet. Even when the text being used was Latin, each verse was still preceded with "*Aleph, Beth, Ghimel...*" Just as in contemporary editions of the Book of Common Prayer one finds the psalms in English, but each psalm is still headed by the old, familiar Latin incipit, for example, *Dixit Dominus Domino meo*. One can see in these archaic elements not just a nostalgia for the way things were, but the need to be catholic in time as well as in space—the sense of holy communion with those who have gone before us.

If, therefore, on Good Friday we find our contemporary Roman Missal preceding the lengthy (by ordinary Sunday morning standards) reading of the passion from John's gospel with a correspondingly lengthy reading from the fifty-second chapter of Isaiah, we can assume a venerable tradition. If we find no less than *twelve* readings still prescribed for our Easter vigil, we can assume that when the proto-Christian communities gathered before dawn to break the bread, they did not limit their scripture selections to our current minimum Sunday-prescribed allowance of three readings. And, of course, if at the other end of the time line we see Paul preaching beyond human endurance, we can see that the fatal temptation to have the homiletic tail wag the scriptural dog is as old as Christianity. Do I hear a Jewish voice saying, "Much older!"?

The fact that these early weekly meetings took place at night, ending at dawn, gave substance to a heartening symbolism. Those early communal readings of the scriptures around, as it were, the foot of the cross, was fittingly enveloped in darkness. Indeed, later gospel accounts would canonize this tradition. The synoptics are at one in recording that when Jesus was dying on the cross, the light died with him. "And when the sixth hour had come, there was darkness over the whole earth until the ninth hour" (Mk 15:33; Mt 27:45; Lk 23:36).[3]

Dark too is the mood of Isaiah's songs of the suffering servant, of the passion of Jeremiah and his Lamentations, of many of the psalms. But the strength of these scriptures is precisely that darkness does not have the last word. Indeed, the psalmist sees this as his task and challenge: "I will awake the dawn" (Ps 57:8). As the night passes, slowly, at first imperceptibly, the faintest glimmer is sensed rather than seen in the east. A world without modern artificial light was more sensitive to this daily miracle, and had a whole series of names for the different gradations of morning light, rather as the Eskimo is said to have many different names for the miracle we call snow. In village and town the first crow of the cock heralded the light, and recalled Peter's denial. But this too is no cause for gloom, for the Petrine tradition looks to the message of the prophets for confirmation, urging the faithful: "You will do well to be attentive to this as to a lamp shining in a dark place, until the day dawns and the morning star rises in your hearts" (2 Pt 1:19). The darkness and the fast would end with the dawn and the breaking of bread.[4]

This has been an attempt to reconstruct something of the unique atmosphere of those early Christian "quilting bees." In earlier chapters the emphasis was on the texts scrutinized in such gatherings. But the quilting was not done by scholars poring with talmudic intensity over texts in a library—sifting, collating, anthologizing. This was theology elaborated on one's knees. It was a theology composed at the foot of the cross, a theology that was closer to the prison than to the library. This was neither a school of metaphysics, nor a system of ethics.[5] This was coping with crucifixion.

9. CRUCIAL CORRESPONDENCE

We preach Christ crucified.[1]

WHILE the more or less systematic searching of the scriptures was yielding its fruits throughout the forties in a nascent oral tradition, the first surviving attempts to address the crucifixion trauma in writing occur in the fifties, in letters attributed, with varying degrees of probability, to "Paul."[2]

Corinth was in those days a cosmopolitan port with a naughty reputation, even by easy-going Greek standards. If the crude crucifixion jokes popular among the rougher elements of Greco-Roman society circulated anywhere, they must surely have been common in the bars and bordellos along the wharves of Corinth. In a letter to the city's novice Christian community Paul grabs the bull by the horns: "Jews demand miraculous signs and Greeks look for wisdom, but we preach Christ crucified: a stumbling block to Jews and an absurdity to pagans" (1 Cor 1:22–23). "For the message of the cross is foolishness to those who are perishing, but to us who are being saved it is the power of God" (1 Cor 1:18).

Upstart Corinth, overshadowed by its glorious neighbor Athens, always had to try harder. Indeed, before escaping to Corinth, Paul had himself received a notably cool reception in the most sophisticated of capitals. Thus rebuffed, Paul adopts a know-nothing pose in the face of Greek pretensions to wisdom *(sophia)*: "For I resolved to know nothing while I was with you except Jesus Christ and him crucified" (1 Cor 2:2).

Paradoxically (and what thoughtful Greek could resist a paradox?) divine strength is to be found in human weakness: "For to be sure, he was crucified in weakness, yet he lives by God's power. Likewise, we are weak in him, yet by God's power we will live with him to serve you" (2 Cor 13:4).

Remarkably, in his *magnum opus* to the community at Rome and in the similar letter to the Galatians, Paul so identifies with Christ that he claims not merely to suffer with Christ, to die with Christ, but to be crucified with Christ: "We know that our old self was crucified with him..." (Rom 6:6). "I have been crucified with Christ and I no longer live, but Christ lives in me" (Gal 2:20). "May I never boast except in the cross of our Lord Jesus Christ, through which the world has been crucified to me, and I to the world" (Gal 6:14).

However, we will not be surprised that not all in a society never far from the terrifying shadow of the cross were convinced by these exalted outpourings, as Paul tearfully acknowledges at a later stage to that community at Philippi that seems to have been closest to him, his "joy and crown": "For, as I have often told you before and now say again even with tears, many live as enemies of the cross of Christ" (Phil 3:18).

An elegant coda to Paul's theology of the cross is offered by the letter to the Hebrews, which most agree was not written by Paul himself: "Let us fix our eyes on Jesus, the author and perfecter of our faith, who for the joy set before him endured the cross, scorning its shame, and sat down at the right hand of the throne of God" (Heb 12:2).

What is remarkable about these texts is that their rabbinical author eschews the quilting approach described above. Instead of seeking support in fulfillment texts, he anticipates Tertullian's "I believe because it is absurd" and the polemical paradoxes of Gilbert Keith Chesterton. Perhaps these letters are geared, if not to gentile readers, certainly to the Jews of the hellenic diaspora long exposed to the seductions of *sophia*. Perhaps it was from such that Paul had himself learned that early hymn to Jesus, which he quotes in his letter to his beloved community at Philippi:

Who, being in very nature God,
did not consider equality with God something to be grasped,
but made himself nothing,
taking *the very nature of a slave*,
being made in human likeness.
And being found in appearance as a man,
he humbled himself
and became obedient to death—
even *death on a cross!*
Therefore God exalted him to the highest place
and gave him the name that is above *every* name,
that at the name of Jesus *every* knee should bow,
in heaven and on earth and under the earth,
and every tongue confess that Jesus Christ is Master,
to the glory of God the Father. (Phil 2:5–11)

This pre-Pauline hymn, possibly composed originally in Aramaic, paints a diptych: Jesus the powerless, ever obedient, dying the death of the slave; Jesus the Supreme Master, the universally venerated Lord, the exalted *Kyrios*.

Other passages explicitly address the Corinthian diaspora's non-negotiable Jewish roots with an appeal to scripture: "For what I received I passed on to you as of first importance: that Christ died for our sins *according to the scriptures*, that he was buried, that he was raised on the third day *according to the scriptures*" (1 Cor 15:3–4).

This is the sum and substance of the Christian message as received by Paul, as passed on by him (tradition). Do many Christians still need reminding that when Paul speaks here of Christ's death and resurrection *according to the scriptures*, the scriptures in question are not Matthew, Mark, Luke and John— books not yet written? For Paul and his audience, the only scriptures were the Hebrew scriptures, probably in Greek translation. Thus Paul and his co-religionists found the story of the death and resurrection of Jesus in the Hebrew scriptures. The repeated *according to the scriptures* is the end product of the "searching of the scriptures" of the Emmaus encounter. One discovery of such a search is spelled out: Christ died *for our sins*.

The community implications of such an atoning death are developed in a later letter to the same Christians of Corinth: "For Christ's love compels us, because we are convinced that one died for all, and therefore all died. And he died for all, that those who live should no longer live for themselves but for him who died for them and was raised again" (2 Cor 5:14–15).

Indeed, in an earlier letter to the fledgling community at Thessalonika, confused and concerned as to the fate of those members who had died before the *Parousia*—the return of Christ then expected as imminent, Paul is reassuring. The scope of Christ's atoning death extends beyond the grave: "He died for us so that, whether we are awake or asleep, we may live together with him" (1 Thess 5:10).

But it is the most enduring biblical image of all that evokes, with marvelous economy, the very birth of Israel out of death: "Christ, our Passover lamb, has been sacrificed" (1 Cor 5:7).

With this image, the emerging Christian tradition taps into the deepest and richest vein of Israel's traditions. This master image sets off a chain reaction of related images: a people despised by an alien culture, persecuted and abused; the lamb "led to the slaughter," enduring in silence; the blood spattered on the wood (of the doorpost, of the cross), to stand between the angel of death and those within; the mass escape from slavery; the journey through sea and desert to the promised land. With the appropriation of this image the Jewish Passover will be co-opted and transformed into the Christian Easter. When today's Christians gather for "the breaking of the bread," they still gratefully intone: "Lamb of God, you take away the sin of the world." This inspired image goes beyond coping.

10. THE GREAT ROMAN TRAUMA

If anyone is ashamed of me...
(See Mk 8:38)

WHILE the initial piecing together of scriptural "quilts" was presumably an oral activity, and while segments may have been later committed to writing, the eventual impulse to publish a more complete synthesis may have been triggered by some third, more *localized*, trauma. In the first century the great *Roman* trauma arguably occurred on July 18, in the year 64:

It began where the Circus adjoins the Palatine and Caelian Hills, where among the taverns stocked with inflammables the fire broke out and gathered strength. It was swept by the wind up the full length of the Circus, since there were neither homes screened by boundary walls nor temples surrounded by stone enclosures, nor barriers of any kind to stop it. The flames raced through the lower quarters first, then shot up the hills, and finally sank back down to finish off their work below, running ahead of all remedial efforts, traveling fast. The city was an easy victim because of the narrow, twisting lanes and winding streets characteristic of old Rome. Add to this the shrieks of terrified women;

51

children running hither and thither; men looking for a way out, drag-
ging the elderly along or stopping to wait for them, in a fatal combi-
nation of hesitation and haste. Many looked behind them, only to be
engulfed from the front or sides. If they made their escape into a
neighboring quarter, that too fell to the flames, and even districts
thought to be out of danger's way were soon in flames. Finally, not
knowing whence or where to run, they flooded the roads or sank
down in the fields. Some who had lost everything chose to die, even
when escape was at hand. They were joined by others who had been
unable to save their loved ones. (Tacitus: *Annales* XV, 38)

Now there was additional cause for grief, and suspicion:

Nobody tried to fight the fire, as there were repeated threats from
many who forbade it, while others openly threw firebrands about
and shouted that they were acting under authority. Maybe they did
this in order to loot the town; maybe they had orders from somebody. (Tacitus: *Annales* XV, 38)

Who could that somebody have been? One could not help noting that the emperor had been conveniently out of town that night,
and had been in no hurry home:

Nero, who at that time was staying in Antium,[1] did not return to the
capital until the fire was nearing the house by which he had connected the Palatine with the Gardens of Maecaenas. It proved
impossible, however, to stop it from engulfing both the Palatine and
the house and all their surroundings. (Tacitus: *Annales* XV, 39)

Nero was already unpopular after a recent and disastrous famine.
Now, despite his opening the imperial gardens to the thousands who
had lost their homes, new rumors fed the city's discontent. "The
rumor spread that, at the very moment when Rome was aflame,
[Nero] had mounted the stage of his private theater to sing the song
of the destruction of Troy"[2] (Tacitus: *Annales* XV, 39).

Other versions of this rumor are found in Suetonius and Dio Cassius, and to this day people who know nothing else of the emperor recognize the phrase: "Nero fiddling while Rome burns."

The fire was finally halted in the usual way. "Only on the sixth day was the fire stopped at the foot of the Esquiline by razing the buildings over a vast area to bar the fire's progress with open ground" (Tacitus: *Annales* XV, 40).

But the respite was short-lived. "Fire broke out again, but in the less crowded quarters. This time while there was less loss of life, there was greater loss of temples and public buildings" (Tacitus: *Annales* XV, 40).

The site of this second fire fed a suspicion already aroused:

The second fire hatched the greater scandal, as it had broken out on the Aemilian property of Tigellinus and appearances suggested that Nero was seeking the glory of founding a new capital and endowing it with his own name. (Tacitus: *Annales* XV, 40)

According to Suetonius, this rebuilt capital was to be called Neronopolis (Ner. 55). And now the capital would indeed have to be rebuilt:

Rome, in fact, is divided into fourteen regions, of which four remained intact, while three were laid level with the ground: in the other seven nothing survived but a few dilapidated and half-burned relics of houses. (Tacitus: *Annales* XV, 40)

The ground was now cleared for Nero to build his dream house, his *Domus Aurea*. Its eventual size may be guaged by the fact that when it was demolished by his successor, Vespasian, the latter's Colosseum is estimated to occupy *one-tenth* of the area of Nero's "Golden House." Before construction could begin, however, Nero had to attend to one little detail:

[Nothing] could stifle scandal or dispel the belief that the fire had taken place by order. Therefore, to scotch the rumor, Nero substituted as culprits, and punished with the utmost refinements of cruelty, a class of men, loathed for their vices, whom the crowd styled Christians. Christus, the founder of the name had undergone the death penalty in the reign of Tiberius, by sentence of the procurator Pontius Pilate, and the pernicious superstition was checked for a moment, only to break out once more, not merely in Judaea, the home of the disease, but in the capital itself, where all things horrible or shameful in the world collect and find a vogue. First, then, the confessed members of the sect were arrested; next, on their disclosures, vast numbers were convicted, not so much on the count of arson as for hatred of the human race. And derision accompanied their end: they were covered with wild beasts' skins and torn to death by dogs...or they were fastened on crosses and, when daylight failed, were burned to serve as lamps by night. (Tacitus: *Annales* XV, 44)

Thus, the specifically Christian trauma, that compounded the trauma of the Great Fire of Rome, was not just the persecution of Christians. Here was a community facing extinction by *crucifixion*. Indeed Peter, their founding father, their living link with Jesus, had been crucified.[3] How could God let this happen? With all the bad news, good news *(evaggelion)* was overdue. A reading public was ripe for "Mark"—the most common male name in Rome.[4] Suddenly coping with crucifixion was no longer the healing of a painful though fading common memory, but an immediate and terrifying need. Never was a theology of the cross more needed than in that Rome (burned? and) rebuilt by Nero:

Then he called the crowd to him along with his disciples and said: "If anyone would come after me, he must deny himself and take up his cross and follow me. For whoever wants to save his life will lose it, but whoever loses his life for me and for the gospel will save it. What good is it for a man to gain the whole world, yet forfeit his soul? Or what can a man give in exchange for his soul? If anyone is ashamed of me and my words in this adulterous and sinful generation, the Son of Man will be ashamed of him when he comes in his Father's glory with the holy angels." (Mk 8:34–38)

As Michael Goulder comments: "Mark's attitude to non-martyrs is quite plain, and it is far from pastoral."[5]

Mark, and Mark alone, drops a tantalizing name in his account of the climb to Golgotha: "A certain man from Cyrene, Simon, the father of Alexander and *Rufus*, was passing by on his way in from the country, and they forced him to carry the cross" (Mk 15:21).

A decade earlier, when Paul wrote to Rome in anticipation of his visit there he concludes the letter with greetings to a twenty-six-name list of members of the Roman community. One name catches the eye: "Greet *Rufus*, chosen in the Lord, and his mother, who has been a mother to me, too" (Rom 16:13). While nothing can be proved, it is tempting to speculate that Rufus was the then-living source of Mark's report of the crucifixion.

One wonders if the rituals of crucifixion as described by Mark were still observed under Nero:

> They brought Jesus to the place called Golgotha (which means The Place of the Skull). Then they offered him wine mixed with myrrh, but he did not take it. And they crucified him. Dividing up his clothes, they cast lots to see what each would get. (Mk 15:22–24)

One suspects that the administration of a narcotic and the confiscation of the clothes and other personal effects were still callously carried out.[6]

As Tacitus reports above of the crucified Christians of Rome, "*derision* accompanied their end." We can imagine the taunts from the police officers, from the judges, from the passers-by, even from ordinary criminals condemned to the same fate:

> It was the third hour when they crucified him. The written notice of the charge against him read: THE KING OF THE JEWS. They crucified two robbers with him, one on his right and one on his left. Those who passed by hurled insults at him, shaking their heads and saying, "So! You who are going to destroy the temple and build it in three days, come down from the cross and save yourself!" In the same way the chief priests and the teachers of the law mocked him

among themselves. "He saved others," they said, "but he can't save himself! Let this Christ, this King of Israel, come down now from the cross, that we may see and believe." Those crucified with him also heaped insults on him. (Mk 15:25–32)

Particularly distressing for Jews and/or Romans for whom the family tomb was sacred was the prospect of being "torn to death by dogs" or being "burned to serve as lamps by night," so that nothing would remain for burial. In their prefight posturing, the worst threats that David and Goliath can make are: "I will give your flesh to the birds of the air and to the wild animals of the field" (Goliath to David); "I will give the dead bodies of the Philistine army this very day to the birds of the air and to the wild animals of the earth" (David to Goliath, Jgs 17:44 and 46). Later in 2 Samuel 20:8–14, David handed seven sons of Saul over to the Gibeonites to be impaled on the mountain. The sister of two of the seven kept watch by the bodies; "she did not allow the birds of the air to come on the bodies by day, or the wild animals by night."[7] When David heard this, he had his people gather the bones of those who had been impaled, along with the bones of Saul and Jonathan whose bodies the Philistines had hung up in the public square of Beth-shan, and buried them in the family tomb. For Jews, a text from Deuteronomy originally referring to hanging came to be applied to crucifixion:

If a man guilty of a capital offense is put to death and his body is hung on a tree, you must not leave his body on the tree overnight. Be sure to bury him that same day, because *anyone who is hung on a tree is under God's curse.* You must not desecrate the land the LORD your God is giving you as an inheritance. (Dt 21:22–23)

The dread of being left unburied, left to be devoured by the birds and the dogs, was connected among many Jews with the fear that thus nothing would be left for the resurrection. We notice that all four gospels are emphatic that such was not the fate of Jesus: he was taken down from the cross and buried in a tomb.

Worst of all was the betrayal of "vast numbers" by their fellow Christians. This is addressed on two levels, perhaps reflecting a debate in the community. The initial reaction is echoed as follows in the Judas story:

> When evening came, Jesus arrived with the Twelve. While they were reclining at the table eating, he said, "I tell you the truth, one of you will betray me—one who is eating with me." They were saddened, and one by one they said to him, "Surely not I?" "It is one of the Twelve," he replied, "one who dips bread into the bowl with me. The Son of Man will go just as it is written about him. But woe to that man who betrays the Son of Man! It would be better for him if he had not been born." (Mk 14:17-21)

In his letter to the Romans, cited above, Paul concludes the long list of greetings to named individuals with "Greet one another with a holy kiss" (Rom 16:16), the traditional seal of Christian fellowship. The enormity of the act of betrayal by a fellow Christian is thus dramatized by Mark: "Now the betrayer had arranged a signal with them: 'The one I kiss is the man; arrest him and lead him away under guard.' Going at once to Jesus, Judas said, 'Rabbi!' and kissed him. The men seized Jesus and arrested him" (Mk 14:44-46).

For the persecuted community, riddled with spies and turncoats, the message is clear: the informer follows in the footsteps of the archbetrayer—Judas. However, alongside the condemnation latent in the Judas story, a more pastoral approach may be discerned in the Peter story:

> Peter declared, "Even if all fall away, I will not." "I tell you the truth," Jesus answered, "today—yes, tonight—before the rooster crows twice you yourself will disown me three times." But Peter insisted emphatically, "Even if I have to die with you, I will never disown you." And all the others said the same. (Mk 14:29-31)

While Peter is selected as the prototype of the betrayer, Mark insists that the other disciples, *all* of them, were no different.

While Peter was below in the courtyard, one of the servant girls of the high priest came by. When she saw Peter warming himself, she looked closely at him. "You also were with that Nazarene, Jesus," she said. But he denied it. "I don't know or understand what you're talking about," he said, and went out into the entryway. When the servant girl saw him there, she said again to those standing around, "This fellow is one of them." Again he denied it. After a little while, those standing near said to Peter, "Surely you are one of them, for you are a Galilean." He began to call down curses on himself, and he swore to them, "I don't know this man you're talking about." Immediately the rooster crowed the second time. Then Peter remembered the word Jesus had spoken to him: "Before the rooster crows twice you will disown me three times." And he broke down and wept. (Mk 14:66–72).

As between the Judas story and the Peter story, which was the more popular in early Rome? If we return to Professor Nardelli's catalog of sculptures[8] in the city's early cemeteries it is no contest:

The kiss of Judas	3
The death of Judas	1
Prophecy of Peter's denial	56

Decades later the fourth gospel will, for another community and in a final chapter which is probably a later-added appendix, complete the rehabilitation of Peter by offsetting his triple denial of Jesus with a triple affirmation of love (Jn 21:15). In the interim both Matthew and Luke will tone down Mark's rough handling of Peter and the other disciples. But for Mark's own community in Rome, no rehabilitation story was necessary. The memory of Peter's own unmentionable death by crucifixion was all too fresh, and indeed preserved in the apocryphal *Acts of Peter*. Significantly, the account opens with the community urging Peter to flee Rome:

...and the rest of the brethren with Marcellus entreated him to withdraw. But Peter said to them, "Shall we act like deserters, brethren?" But they said to him, "No, it is so you can go on serving the Lord." So he assented to the brethren and withdrew by himself, saying, "Let none of you retire with me, but I shall retire by myself in disguise." And as he went out of the gate he saw the Lord entering Rome; and when he saw him he said, "Lord, where are you going?" And the Lord said to him, "I am coming to Rome to be crucified again." And Peter came to himself; and he saw the Lord ascending into heaven; then he returned to Rome, rejoicing and giving praise to the Lord, because he said, "I am being crucified"; since this was to happen to Peter.[9]

After comforting the community, Peter is then arrested, hauled before the prefect, duly condemned and taken to the place of execution, where the text turns lyrical:

> Then when he had approached and stood by the cross he began to say, "O name of the cross, mystery that is concealed! O grace ineffable that is spoken in the name of the cross! O nature of man that cannot be parted from God! O love, unspeakable and inseparable, that cannot be disclosed through unclean lips! I seize you now, being come to the need of my release from here. I will declare you, what you are; I will not conceal the mystery of the cross that has long been enclosed and hidden from my soul. You who hope in Christ, for you the cross must not be this thing that is visible; for this passion, like the passion of Christ, is something other than this which is visible....I request you therefore, executioners, to crucify me head downwards—in this way and no other. And the reason I will tell to those who hear."[10]

Peter, hanged in the manner requested, launches into a somewhat elaborate symbolic explanation: "...the first man, whose likeness I have in my appearance, in falling head downwards, showed a manner of birth that was not so before...."

Hence the crucifixion of Jesus is, so to speak, "revolutionary":

> You then, my beloved, both those who hear me now and those that shall hear in time, must leave your former error and turn back again; for you should come up to the cross of Christ, who is the Word stretched out, the one and only, of whom the spirit says, "For what else is Christ but the Word, the sound of God?" So that the Word is this upright tree

on which I am crucified; but the sound is the cross-piece, the nature of man; and the nail that holds the cross-piece to the upright in the middle is the conversion [or turning point] and repentance of man.[11]

We have here a crucifixion symbolism too strained for our current taste, and perhaps even for the tastes of that time, since this work remained apocryphal. The touching legend of the encounter with Jesus remained in Christian folklore, and there are an impressive forty sculptures of *The Flight of Peter* in early Roman cemeteries,[12] but the overly contrived paean to crucifixion is forgotten.

Moreover, as Paul reports with exasperation, local communities tended to elevate their founding father to cult status:

> My brothers, some from Chloe's household have informed me that there are quarrels among you. What I mean is this: One of you says, "I follow Paul"; another, "I follow Apollos"; another, "I follow Cephas"; still another, "I follow Christ." (1 Cor 1:11–12)

Who can have been more likely to eclipse a Jesus who had never set foot in Rome than Rome's very own Cephas/Peter? Moreover, in the very next line of the above letter to Corinth, Paul gets carried off by his own cross-centered rhetoric: "Is Christ divided? *Was Paul crucified for you?* Were you baptized in the name of Paul?" (1 Cor 1:11–12)

Once we transpose for Roman consumption the italicized question to *Was Cephas crucified for you?* then it becomes obvious that Paul's rhetoric creates more problems than it solves.

An ancient tradition has it that after his crucifixion Peter was buried on the Vatican hill, and across the centuries pilgrims have traveled there to venerate his tomb. *Mark* may have wished to apply an early corrective. No man is a hero to his own "interpreter." Ultimately, then, as one commentator puts it:

> Mark's message is as clear as it is simple. No one can confess that Jesus is the Son of God until he has acknowledged the crucified Messiah. No one can be Jesus' disciple unless he accepts the scan-

dal of the cross. The passion narrative is the climax of Mark's Gospel because it is the moment when the secret of Jesus' identity is fully revealed. It is the proper understanding of this secret that makes discipleship possible.[13]

Noting that *Mark's* text contains a greater proportion of miraculous cures (24 percent of the text) than do the texts of his successors, it has been suggested that *Mark* is targeting those who reduce Jesus to just another wonderworker and look to him to cure all their ills. Not so, says the Jesus of Mark: "If anyone would come after me, he must deny himself and take up his cross and follow me" (Mk 8:34).

Again, the triumphant post-death appearances of Jesus that conclude the other three gospels blind us to the fact that *Mark's* original austere version of the Good News ended in a climate of alarm, bewilderment and fear:

> As they entered the tomb, they saw a young man dressed in a white robe sitting on the right side, and *they were alarmed*. "Don't be alarmed," he said. "You are looking for Jesus the Nazarene, who was crucified. He has risen! He is not here. See the place where they laid him. But go, tell his disciples and Peter, 'He is going ahead of you into Galilee. There you will see him, just as he told you.'" *Trembling and bewildered*, the women went out and fled from the tomb. They said nothing to anyone, because *they were afraid*. (Mk 16:5–8)

The Rome of Nero must have been for the fledgling Christian community a city of alarm, bewilderment and fear. The messenger at the perplexingly empty tomb tries to reassure them: "Don't be alarmed." But, at least initially, his words seem to compound the anxiety, and for the time being fear has the last word.

Needless to say, this was too challenging for many readers, and the usual "improvers" lost little time in adding standard stories of post-death appearances by Jesus, cobbled together from other sources to make a more fitting conclusion to *Mark*. Indeed, within a decade or two *Mark* would come to be rewritten from beginning to end by Matthew and Luke with the addition of much new material, so that St. Augustine would consider *Mark* redundant, and the Lectionary of the Tridentine Missal would continue to evidence *Mark's* partial eclipse until the liturgical reform of Vatican II. Already in Nero's Rome, for most people *Mark's* message of the cross cut too close to the bone. His recent revival (academic and liturgical) may suggest that his is still a powerful message for an age of anxiety.

11. JEWS FOR JESUS— DOUBLE TRAUMA

Destroy this temple and in three days I will raise it up.[1]

AFTER the fall of Jerusalem in A.D. 70 we have an overlap of two traumatized groups—constituting a third group that suffers from a double trauma: as Jesus People coping with crucifixion, as Jews coping with the destruction of the temple. Indeed the extent of the overlap can be guaged in part from the report by Tacitus of the wartime debate between Romans as to whether the second temple should be destroyed. Those against destruction counseled Roman (stoic) moderation. Those for it argued, "It would result in the utter destruction of the Jews and the Christians, who, though hostile to each other, had a common origin. The Christians stemmed from the Jews. Hence if you tore up the roots (i.e., destroyed the temple), the whole plant would perish."

While the crucifixion of Jesus and the destruction of the temple seem totally independent of one another, in the minds of these Jewish Jesus People searching for answers in the scriptures, the two historically separate events begin to converge. This convergence will ultimately surface in that Book of Signs we find incorporated into the

fourth gospel.[2] There Jesus goes up to the temple just before
Passover and drives the money-changers from the temple.[3] Our
Bibles describe this as the *cleansing* of the temple. But the term
"cleansing" appears nowhere in the text, and in view of the subse-
quent dialogue, this violent attack[4] seems a biblical sign,[5] a prophecy
in action, a symbolic *destruction* of the temple. For when the Jews
ask him: "What sign can you show us for doing this? Jesus answers:
"*Destroy* this temple and in three days I will raise it up." As usual in
the fourth gospel, this enigmatic answer only puzzles the audience
further. "This temple has been under construction for forty-six
years,[6] and you will raise it up in three days?" The evangelist
explains: "But he was speaking of the temple of his body." Thus for
that generation of Jewish Jesus People, the death of Jesus and the
destruction of the temple were telescoped into the one traumatic
event. For *John as for Luke,* such insight by hindsight would not
come until after the resurrection and the Jesus-illuminated searching
of the scriptures. "After he was raised from the dead, his disciples
recalled what he had said. Then they believed the Scripture and the
words that Jesus had spoken."

For followers of Jesus, moreover, the destruction of the second
temple should not be the end of their world, since temples had
become redundant:

> "Sir," the woman said, "I can see that you are a prophet. Our fathers
> worshiped on this mountain, but you Jews claim that the place where
> we must worship is in Jerusalem." Jesus declared, "Believe me,
> woman, a time is coming when you will worship the Father neither on
> this mountain nor in Jerusalem. You Samaritans worship what you do
> not know; we worship what we do know, for salvation is from the
> Jews. Yet a time is coming and has now come when the true wor-
> shipers will worship the Father in spirit and truth, for they are the kind
> of worshipers the Father seeks. God is spirit, and his worshipers must
> worship in spirit and in truth." (Jn 4:19–24)

The prominence of this and other Samaritan allusions in the fourth
gospel has led many to speculate that the Johannine community

included a Samaritan component.[7] The Samaritans were essentially Israelites who stayed north of Jerusalem while other Israelites were packed off into exile in Babylon. To keep their faith alive "in an alien land" the exiles had to reinvent it. When seventy years later they returned to Jerusalem with their reminted beliefs, they came to see their old, more tradition-bound, neighbors as heretics. The feeling was mutual. The result was two competing confessions, with two collections of sacred scriptures, two temples, and fanatical hatred. This hatred is epitomized in John 8:48: "The Jews answered him, 'Aren't we right in saying that you are a Samaritan and demon-possessed?'" Hence the astonishment of the woman at the well in John 4:9: "The Samaritan woman said to him, 'You are a Jew and I am a Samaritan woman. How can you ask me for a drink?' (For Jews do not associate with Samaritans.)" The point is that it took Jesus to reveal the good news that such dreary confessional squabblings had been transcended by a spirit that defies local containment.

Contemporary concern that the second temple might be destroyed is reflected in a rabbinic tradition that Rabbi Zadok began fasting about A.D. 30 to forestall the destruction of Jerusalem. Particularly interesting are the actions and fate of a later Jesus:

> There was one Jesus, the son of Ananus, a plebeian and a husbandman, who, for years before the war began, and at a time when the city was in very great peace and prosperity, came to that feast whereon it is our custom for everyone to make tabernacles to God in the temple, and began on a sudden to cry aloud, "A voice from the east, a voice from the west, a voice from the four winds, a voice against Jerusalem and the holy house, a voice against the bridegrooms and the brides, and a voice against this whole people!" This was his cry, as he went about by day and by night, in all the lanes of the city. However, certain of the most eminent among the populace had great indignation at this dire cry of his, and took up the man, and gave him a great number of severe stripes; yet he did not either say anything for himself, or anything peculiar to those that chastised him, but still he went on with the same words which he cried before. Hereupon our rulers supposing, as the case proved to be, that there was a sort of

divine fury in the man, brought him to the Roman procurator, where he was whipped till his bones were laid bare; yet did he not make any supplication for himself, nor shed any tears, but turning his voice to the most lamentable tone possible, at every stroke of the whip, his answer was, "Woe, woe to Jerusalem!" And when Albinus, for he was then our procurator, asked him who he was, and whence he came, and why he uttered such words, he made no manner of reply to what he said, but still did not leave his melancholy ditty, till Albinus took him to be a madman, and dismissed him. Now during all the time that passed before the war began, this man did not go near any of the citizens, nor was seen by them while he said so; but he every day uttered these lamentable words, as if it were his premeditated vow, "Woe, woe, to Jerusalem!" Nor did he give ill words to those that beat him every day, nor good words to those that gave him food; but this was his reply to all men, and indeed no other than a melancholy presage of what was to come. This cry of his was the loudest at the festivals; and he continued this ditty for seven years and five months, without growing hoarse, or being tired therewith, until the very time that he saw his presage in earnest fulfilled in our siege, when it ceased; for as he was going round upon the wall, he cried out with the utmost force, "Woe, woe, to the city again, and to the people, and to the holy house!" And just as he added at the last, "Woe, woe, to myself also!" there came a stone out of one of the engines, and as he was uttering the very same presages, he gave up the ghost. [Josephus: *The Wars of the Jews* VI, 5, 300 ff.]

Like Jesus of Nazareth, Jesus bar Ananus chose the feast days to announce the destruction of city and temple. Irate Jews turned both over to the Roman procurator who, frustrated by their refusal to answer questions, tried to whip sense into them.

This illustrates that in such a milieu one did not have to receive a special revelation from on high to know that by behaving as he behaved, by speaking as he spoke, Jesus of Nazareth would inevitably excite nationalistic fervor among his compatriots, attract the attention of the (Jewish) temple police, and wind up before a Roman tribunal where any attempt at theological explanations would be useless in the face of Roman *realpolitik*. Indeed, one could confidently predict many of the details of how such a prisoner would be treated by his military captors (their standard sadistic games), by the Sanhedrin (the standard mock trial with the set piece by the high priest), by the procurator (the standard scourging).

12. EX-JEWS FOR JESUS—
THE EXPULSION TRAUMA

...for already the Jews had decided that anyone who acknowledged that Jesus was the Christ would be put out of the synagogue.[1]

WE have earlier intimated that the fall of the temple led to the expansion of the synagogue. In point of fact, such an evolution was already in preparation before the destruction of the second temple. The diaspora saw the construction of synagogues throughout the cities of the Roman Empire, so that Paul's journeys criss-cross the imperial map from synagogue to synagogue. There was even a rival temple built in Egypt. Indeed, for those purists the Essenes, the second temple with its non-Aaronic priesthood had already been *superseded* by the council of the community: "*A house of holiness for Israel...a most holy dwelling for Aaron...and shall offer up sweet fragrance...*"[2] While Jews from all over, including "strangers from Rome," still thronged Jerusalem during the major feasts, according to Luke, there must have been many more Jews who did not make the trip the prescribed three times a year. Moreover, while Luke's Jesus People at the end of volume one "returned to Jerusalem with great joy, and they were continually in the temple blessing God" (24:53), and volume two's opening section shows them spending "much time together in the temple," this is for prayer and teaching. They are not depicted as taking place in those uniquely temple rites—the sacrifices. Instead, "they broke bread at home" (2:46). So while for all Jews, whether in the homeland or in the diaspora, the destruction of the temple was a great calamity, thanks to their local synagogues they could regroup.

The local trauma that triggered the bulk of the Johannine literature would seem to have been the final and irreversible expulsion of Jewish Jesus People from their synagogues.

For Jesus People who were Jews, and determined to remain Jews in the ultra-orthodox synagogues of the postwar period, the question, *Why crucifixion?* had already found a *Mosaic* answer:

> Just as Moses lifted up the snake in the desert, so the Son of Man must be lifted up, that everyone who believes in him may have eternal life. For God so loved the world that he gave his one and only Son, that whoever believes in him shall not perish but have eternal life (Jn 3:14–16).

Interestingly, verse 16 is often quoted all by itself as being the heart of the fourth gospel. When restored to its immediate context it is seen to spring from the specifically Johannine/Mosaic theology of the cross.

As for the fresh shock of expulsion from the synagogue:

> They brought to the Pharisees the man who had been blind. Now the day on which Jesus had made the mud and opened the man's eyes was a Sabbath. Therefore the Pharisees also asked him how he had received his sight. "He put mud on my eyes," the man replied, "and I washed, and now I see." Some of the Pharisees said, "This man is not from God, for he does not keep the Sabbath." But others asked, "How can a sinner do such miraculous signs?" So they were divided. Finally they turned again to the blind man, "What have you to say about him? It was your eyes he opened." The man replied, "He is a prophet." The Jews still did not believe that he had been blind and had received his sight until they sent for the man's parents. "Is this your son?" they

asked. "Is this the one you say was born blind? How is it that now he can see?" "We know he is our son," the parents answered, "and we know he was born blind. But how he can see now, or who opened his eyes, we don't know. Ask him. He is of age; he will speak for himself." His parents said this because *they were afraid of the Jews, for already the Jews had decided that anyone who acknowledged that Jesus was the Christ would be put out of the synagogue.* That was why his parents said, "He is of age; ask him." A second time they summoned the man who had been blind. "Give glory to God," they said. "We know this man is a sinner." He replied, "Whether he is a sinner or not, I don't know. One thing I do know. I was blind but now I see!" Then they asked him, "What did he do to you? How did he open your eyes?" He answered, "I have told you already and you did not listen. Why do you want to hear it again? Do you want to become his disciples, too?" Then they hurled insults at him and said, "You are this fellow's disciple! We are disciples of Moses! We know that God spoke to Moses, but as for this fellow, we don't even know where he comes from." The man answered, "Now that is remarkable! You don't know where he comes from, yet he opened my eyes. We know that God does not listen to sinners. He listens to the godly man who does his will. Nobody has ever heard of opening the eyes of a man born blind. If this man were not from God, he could do nothing." To this they replied, "You were steeped in sin at birth; how dare you lecture us!" *And they threw him out.* Jesus heard that they had thrown him out, and when he found him, he said, "Do you believe in the Son of Man?" "Who is he, sir?" the man asked. "Tell me so that I may believe in him." Jesus said, "You have now seen him; in fact, he is the one speaking with you." Then the man said, "Lord, I believe," and he worshiped him. Jesus said, "For judgment I have come into this world, so that the blind will see and those who see will become blind." Some Pharisees who were with him heard him say this and asked, "What? Are we blind too?" Jesus said, "If you were blind, you would not be guilty of sin; but now that you claim you can see, your guilt remains." (Jn 9:13–41)

The reader will pardon the long quote, but the typically Johannine interplay of elements is such that any editing is an immediate impoverishment. The Jew born blind and in sin is illuminated and washed clean by Christian baptism. With his new sight, he sees Jesus as a prophet, which is threatening to the followers of *the* prophet, Moses. So the synagogue throws him out. His family would also be thrown out, but they studiously dissociate themselves from the black sheep. At the end the Pharisees, from whose ranks emerged the rabbis of the postwar reform, are the truly blind. The jaunty attitude of the blind man (who probably never really belonged, anyway!) is totally uncharacteristic. For most, the prospect of excommunication was terrifying:

> Yet at the same time many even among the leaders believed in him. But because of the Pharisees *they would not confess their faith for fear they would be put out of the synagogue;* for they loved praise from men than praise from God. (Jn 12:42–43)

This last phrase is hardly fair. Members of the synagogue had a lot more to lose than empty praise. The synagogue was their whole world. Without it their businesses would fail, their children would be unmarriageable, their identity lost, their very lives in jeopardy. Given the degree to which today's mainline Christians are integrated into secular society, the sanction of excommunication offers no helpful parallel. For this we have to turn to the Old Order Amish:

> The ultimate sanction is the imposition of the *Meidung*, also known as the "shunning," or "ban."... the ban is total. No one in the district is allowed to associate with the errant party, including members of his or her own family. Even normal marital relations are forbidden. Should any member of the community ignore the *Meidung*, that person would also be placed under the ban.[3]

Perhaps the current casualties of corporate downsizing present a more familiar model: the ignominious firing, the loss of identity, the disappearance of security, the economic spiral, the contempt of one's enemies, the foreclosure on the home, the family shame, the divorce, the drinking, finally joining the homeless on the cold streets, as chillingly documented in a series of articles in the *New York Times* in April 1996.

For Jesus People who were also members of these newly reformed postwar synagogues, the temptation to hold back from the increasingly uncompromising Johannine "Way" would be well-nigh irresistible:

> All this I have told you so that you will not go astray. *They will put you out of the synagogue*; in fact, a time is coming when anyone who kills you will think he is offering a service to God. They will do such things because they have not known the Father or me. I have told you this, so that when the time comes you will remember that I warned you. (Jn 16:1–4)[4]

Such mass excommunications, and occasional deaths, led the Johannine community to add a new and fatal element to their already developed theology of the cross: sole responsibility for the crucifixion of Jesus rests on the Jews (a term used 70 times in the fourth gospel, as opposed to the five or six times in the synoptics[5]).

A further trauma of a more domestic nature for what we now call the Johannine community was the death of their "Beloved Disciple."

> Peter turned and saw that the disciple whom Jesus loved was following them. (This was the one who had leaned back against Jesus at the supper and had said, "Lord, who is going to betray you?") When Peter saw him, he asked, "Lord, what about him?" Jesus answered, "If I want him to remain alive until I return, what is that to you? You must follow me." Because of this, the rumor spread among the brothers that this disciple would not die. But Jesus did not say that he would not die; he only said, "If I want him to remain alive until I return, what is that to you?" This is the disciple who testifies to these things and who wrote them down. We know that his testimony is true. (Jn 21:20–24)

For his own community, the death of the Beloved Disciple was unthinkable. Certain words of Jesus lent color to a rumor of immortality, making the eventual death all the more perplexing. But the rumor is exposed as resting on a misreading of the words of Jesus. Thus, a community "tradition" with a small "t" is given decent burial. A lesson for all Christian communities.

13. CONSTANTINE: THE CROSS CO-OPTED?

In hoc signo vinces.

FROM Nero (A.D. 37–68) through Diocletian (A.D. 245–316) persecution of Christians was intermittent. Its revival under Diocletian was oblique. The new emperor, like most of his predecessors, could thank the military for bringing him to power. However, this only served to show that an army that made emperors could unmake them. Hence a renewed attempt to invest the imperial purple with a divine aura. Coins were struck that emphasized Diocletian's special relationship with Jupiter. Palace protocol was elaborated to impose ritual prostrations on all admitted to the imperial presence. Imperial devotion to the gods, particularly Mithras (favored by the military) was revived.

A decree in 296 lashed out at "...the malicious obstinacy of base men who displace the old worship of the gods by unprecedented sects in order to make an end of that which was once delivered to us from the gods." The immediate target of this decree, promulgated in Alexandria, was the Persian sect of the Manichees, then spreading westward. "There is reason to fear that in the course of time the unbridled practices and perverted laws of these Persians will poison innocent persons, the sober and peaceable Roman people and indeed the entire globe." Among these "perverted laws" was a prohibition against bearing children, based on the notion that thereby more souls were imprisoned in bodies. The Manichean leaders and their writings were to be burned, their followers executed, their property confiscated.

It was only a matter of time before Christians fell afoul of the new policies. Sacrifices to the old gods became mandatory for court officials, then for army officers, then for common soldiers. When Christians balked at this, a further series of decrees escalated the penalties into a full-blown persecution of Christians. It was, however, too late to turn back the religious clock. The resultant climate of fear pervading the administration and the army was oppressive for Christian and non-Christian alike. It eroded the positive reforms introduced by Diocletian, and by the year 305 he found himself obliged to resign in favor of his colleague Galerius, who had been most zealous in fomenting Diocletian's anti-Christian policies. It was therefore ironic that Galerius should be impelled to issue an Edict of Toleration in 311—a public admission that the last stand for the old gods had failed.

While the persecutions had varied in intensity from decade to decade and from place to place, perhaps the most wounding by-product was the division in the community as to how much one should resist imperial demands. Thus, when a decree ordered the confiscation of the sacred scriptures, one bishop cheerfully handed over a shelf of medical treatises, while another got rid of heretical works he had been keeping out of harm's way. This scandalized some members of the latter's flock, who denounced him and went off to prison to show what real Christians are made of. The furious bishop saw this as pointless provocation, and sent his archdeacon to the prison to prevent others from bringing food to these self-appointed confessors of the faith. Such personality clashes would inevitably find *theological* sanction, and harden into full-blown schism.[1] This very controversy between those who preferred confrontation to those who sank down roots while bowing to the storm had left the important see of Carthage after A.D. 311 with two rival communities headed by two rival bishops.

But by 312 a drastic change occurred. That was the year that Constantine descended on Rome to attack Maxentius, his rival for the imperial crown.[2] With monumental stupidity Maxentius emerged from behind the city walls and, with the Tiber at his back, engaged Constantine's inferior force. Maxentius was routed, and drowned in the Tiber. The huge Arch of Constantine, with its scenes of this Battle of the Milvian Bridge, still stands by the Colosseum. The *Vita Constantini* of Eusebius of Caesarea tells the story of the legendary vision that appeared in the sky before the battle: "The form of a cross with an impression in stars, in Latin letters, declaring to the emperor Constantine, *In this, conquer.*" Public perception of the cross was about to change drastically.

> The first action of the God-promoted emperor after gaining control of Rome was to order the remains of the holy martyrs to be collected and given consecrated burial; then he commanded that all prosecutions of Christians should be annulled and those in exile should be recalled, those in prison should be released, and those whose property had been confiscated should have it restored, and the church of God would be rebuilt with much zeal and costly offerings....When the Romans saw these things, they rejoiced and were very glad, and observed a festival for seven days to thank God for the victory; and they began to worship the venerable Cross of the Lord and bow down to it and salute it, and they extolled Constantine as a conqueror famed in song and story.[3]

What would the shade of Alexander, still haunting the schoolroom on the Palatine Hill, have made of it all? But this was only the beginning. Crucifixion was abolished, and a decree of 316 directed that prisoners were no longer to be branded on the face, "because [humans are] made in God's image." Imperial funds were lavished on the Roman shrines of Peter and Paul, and churches built in Bethlehem and at the Holy Sepulcher. Constantine's mother traveled to Palestine, where she is said to have found the actual cross and nails used to crucify Jesus. Universal devotion to the Holy Cross was on its way.

Coping with crucifixion was no longer a problem. The church must now cope with Constantine. An emperor who was paying the bills was not going to be a mere spectator when it came to church affairs. He was particularly disturbed by the divisions in the church, by Donatism in the West and Arianism in the East. Anxious to heal political divisions and consolidate the hard-won unity of the empire after yet another civil war, a state religion would help greatly.

What were the current choices? The austere tenets of Stoicism were clearly for the high-minded few. The old emperor-worship, always more popular in the East than in the West, had been debased by officialdom. Mithraism never looked beyond its narrow appeal, chiefly to the military. What, then, of Christianity? Constantine's mother was a devout Christian, his father easily tolerant. Diocletian's persecution had petered out in obvious failure, like all the others. Christianity's teachings may well have appealed to an emperor who was in his private life notably chaste and sober, one who outlawed the savagery of the amphitheater, and who did more for the slave, the foundling and the oppressed than any other emperor.

But if Christianity were to play a role in consolidating the empire, it must first heal its own divisions. When a great council was convened at Ancyra, Constantine transferred the site to Nicea so that he could personally control the proceedings. And control he did. From Constantine's perspective, there were two requirements. First, the church council should be ecumenical. The recent proliferation of local councils could be confusing. As many bishops as possible must be convoked, and from all across the empire. Indeed, to ensure maximum and timely attendance, they would travel at imperial expense. Second, the resultant decisions and decrees should be unanimous, or as close to unanimous as practical. A show of unity—that is what the church and the empire needed. Accordingly, at the council itself, Constantine set the tone by burning, unread, the letters he had received from various bishops charging various brother bishops of conduct unbecoming a bishop. He preached a sermon on unity. Indeed, he seemed to care little about the esoteric details of the main debate, the attempt to articulate the mystery of God's incarnation in the man Jesus.[4]

A significant feature of Constantine's reign was his building of many magnificent churches. In Jerusalem the church of the Holy Sepulcher was preeminent, followed by a second at the cave of the nativity in Bethlehem, and a third on the Mount of Olives. The Holy City was being developed into a center of pilgrimage. Some ten Roman churches, including St. John Lateran and St. Peter's, are traced back to Constantine and his family. A standard feature of these monumental structures was the erection of crosses inside and out. A century before Constantine, the Christian Minucius Felix had protested: "We neither honor nor do we need crosses."[5] A century after Constantine, Nilus was grumbling at an unseemly proliferation of crosses, *maintaining* that one cross in the apse was enough.[6]

It was at the now traditional site of the Holy Sepulcher in Jerusalem that Constantine's mother found the original cross of Jesus. Given the prevailing climate, such a find was probably just a question of time. Splinters were distributed throughout what was fast becoming Christendom. Now associated with victory, the cross found its way onto the battle standards of the nations. "With the Cross of Christ and in the name of Jesus we go into battle brave through this sign, through the banner unflinching," trumpeted Ambrose, fourth-century bishop of Milan.[7] Today Britain's Union Jack bears three overlapping crosses for good measure. Both Helena and Constantine are celebrated as saints in the Greek Orthodox calendar.

Historians predictably ask whether this Constantinian church was an improvement on its predecessor. In the former German Democratic Republic (East Germany), many Lutheran churches had become centers of courageous resistance to a godless regime. After the Berlin Wall came down so did church attendance. One local pastor was asked: "Not many came this Sunday. Where are the others?" "Ach," was the sad reply, "they are probably gone window-shopping over in West Berlin." With the advent of Constantine, the Christians finally emerged from the catacombs and went window-shopping all over Rome. Converts were quick to jump on the imperial bandwagon. In one generation, the cross went from badge of infamy to token of opportunism.

14. CONCLUSION: COPING WITH CRUCIFIXION

Out there in Jutland
In the old man-killing parishes
I will feel lost,
Unhappy and at home.[1]

WHEN a group's world comes to an end, if the group is to survive its immune system must kick in to adapt the body to the new environment. For those Jews who were Jesus People, the prime constituent of their collective immune system was those scriptures that were a peculiar product of a prior period of temple destruction and exile; this was their genetic antidote to loss of belief. This essay has sought to trace the successive steps in their brilliantly successful attempt to cope with the crucifixion, to forge a new identity, to wrest lasting victory from ignominious defeat.

This writer has, of course, no evidence that our four canonical gospels evolved in the general manner suggested above. He has clearly been hypnotized by his gazing at the pages of scripture until he thinks he sees certain suggestive patterns. The occasional references (readily multipliable) to contemporary and ancient writers would indicate that he is not the first to be so seduced. As an appellate lawyer he is trained to reconstruct the story from the police reports, the probation reports, the statements of witnesses, the transcripts of the trial, the recollections of the defendant and of his trial counsel. While this sifting and collating is always an absorbing exercise, this writer is the first to note that his reconstructions and conclusions have invariably and significantly differed from those of the Attorney General! He can only submit his brief and ask for a fair hearing.

A recent, more teutonically systematic review of the early church's varied efforts to explain the death of Jesus concludes that there were many different answers; that none of these answers dropped down from above; that they evidence the church's repeated attempts to rethink its understanding of the death of Jesus, that each "explanation" has its strengths and weaknesses, and that these varied explanations are not reducible to a closed synthesis.[2] In short, a work in progress within a church which was itself a work in progress.

There remains a question that will have occurred to the reader very early in this presentation: how much of the passion narratives are woven out of whole cloth (the Jewish scriptures), and how much is historical in our seven-o'clock-news sense? Scholars differ. Most opt for a considerable degree of editorial license, as would seem evidenced by the sheer bulk of scriptural references found in the passion narratives. Here the words of a distinguished journalist reviewing a couple of recent histories of the Vietnam War may be less surprising on reflection than at first sight: "After covering some wars myself, moreover, I have reached the conclusion that truthful history is often more effectively revealed in works of fiction than in factual journalism."[3] Dominic Crossan claims, against the reservations of Raymond E. Brown,[4] that the disciples knew nothing of what happened once Jesus was arrested and taken away, and classifies the resurrection stories as "damage control." For my own part, noting the presence of "servants" in the household of Herod and of the procurator I suggest that where there are servants close to the seat of power, there is gossip. And I am confident that there was never more gossip than on that particular Passover. That being said, where one comes down on the, by now, inevitable fundamentalist-reductionist spectrum may be due to a perplexing function of vested interests and psychological predisposition. Fortunately, faith in Christ does not hinge on knowledge of what precisely happened to him after his arrest, beyond the consecrated formula: "...suffered under Pontius Pilate, died and was buried; the third day he arose again, *according to the scriptures*...." All the rest is loving embroidery—a family heirloom, rightly treasured, and a comfort to many of us in the current long winter of our deconstruction.

For the present writer a much more puzzling phenomenon than the extensive recycling of the Old Testament into the New is the following. A recent *New York Times* piece compared the situation of the church in Japan and China. The early Japanese church was most brutally persecuted, with crucifixion being only one of the forms of the most refined tortures. The Christian communities persevered heroically, secretly hanging on to their beliefs and practices even after all priests had been killed or expelled. Today, under a regime of benign indifference, the children of these tenacious Christians are quietly dropping out. A less extreme example is afforded by the decline in church practice in Poland since the collapse of communism. In China, by contrast, where persecution of Christians has lately been renewed, the church is experiencing a remarkable growth. (One is reminded of the dry observation of Horace Walpole, when the Grand Lodge found itself under assault in 1734, that the Freemasons were in such low repute that "nothing but a persecution could bring them into vogue again.")

At the conclusion of our essay, such reports prompt a perplexing question. *Has Christianity invested so heavily into coping with crucifixion that it cannot cope without it?* That nostalgia for the good old days of persecution is not restricted to Christianity, or indeed to religion, is shown by a recent review of Jewish polymath George Steiner's *Errata: An Examined Life.* "His compulsive earnestness leads him (with suitable disclaimers) to admit to a sneaking nostalgia for the former Soviet bloc. In its bizarre way, he argues, Stalin's persecution of poets represented a tribute to the power of the word, a power it has lost in the illiterate democracies."

The immediate post-Constantinian era saw the early flowering of monasticism. In their prophetic *fuga mundi*, their flight from the seductions of the city to the austere and challenging landscape of the desert, the radical Christians embraced hardship. *Per crucem ad lucem* (by way of the cross to the light). In the post-Constantinian church monks were not the only Christians, but they were unquestionably the real thing. By their lifestyle they took issue with two imperial imperatives: the payment of taxes (Constantine closed many loopholes) and military service (Constantine made a sweeping reorganization of the army). To what extent they were a countercultural movement, opting out of Constantine's church, is a matter of debate. But it is on record that occasionally their confrontations with local bishops grew violent and imperial troops had to be sent in to restore order.

After the New Testament there can be few books more seminal in the history of Christianity than the sixth-century *Rule for Monks* attributed to St. Benedict. On the one hand its influence extended beyond the monastery walls, in that monks were largely the remakers of "Christendom" after the collapse of the Roman Empire. A recognizable form of the black, hooded monastic cowl is still worn by the judge on the bench, the professor at the rostrum. On the other hand, the *Rule* had no pretensions of originality, other than being an inspired restatement of certain principles of the gospel carried to conclusions that were at once breathtakingly sublime and eminently practical. Chapter 49 of the Rule, *On the Observance of Lent*, opens with the observation: "The life of a monk ought to be a *continuous* Lent."

Lent is still the most dynamic time of the liturgical year. What little obligatory fast and abstinence remains is concentrated in this period. The Sunday liturgies lead inexorably toward the grand climax of the *triduum sacrum*, where the reading of the passion narrative and the adoration of the cross never fail to stir feelings long dormant. But when the forty days of Lent are over and the fifty days of Eastertide begin, instead of changing gear upward we seem to shift back down to automatic pilot.

Is it because we can more readily identify with pain and suffering, with death and desolation, than with ease and joy, with resurrection and life? Yes indeed, how many people can cope with joy? Is that why there is so little of it?

I once knew a man who intrigued me. He was the ultimate worrywart. I would reassure him on one score, but he would be back in two days with another worry, equally groundless. I would reassure him anew. The cycle continued. After each of my reassurances he would be physically transformed with relief: "Oh, thank God. That's wonderful. Then there's no problem, after all. Thank you, thank you, thank you." Finally it dawned on me. He never knew joy. His substitute was *relief*. He got his fix by inventing pseudo-crises. After years of practice, and with more than a dash of paranoia, he was expert. Progress was stumbling from non-crisis to non-crisis, fueled by regular intoxicating infusions of sheer *relief*. Our man was hooked on relief. An extreme example of inability to cope with joy.

On a social level, this seems to translate into *Schadenfreude*. "Laugh and the world laughs with you," says the proverb, "cry, and you cry alone." Not so! I have long observed that when tragedy strikes, your friends rally round. When you are down, people simply can't do enough for you. But if you enjoy some unprecedented success, there is often an eerie silence. Born and bred in Ireland, I used to think this was a perverse Irish quality. It is. But on comparing notes with a Chinese client I discovered she was painfully familiar with the same phenomenon, both home in Kowloon and here in San Francisco's Chinatown. "Rejoice with those who rejoice; mourn with those who mourn," urges St. Paul. Oddly, the latter precept seems more congenial to most than the former.

If joy is the fruit of the Spirit, it would seem the Spirit has a hard time setting down roots in many hearts. The *Palestinian Talmud* warns that in the world to come we will be answerable for the pleasures we have not enjoyed. This, and the parable of the talents, may serve to remind us that at the Final Judgment "coping with crucifixion" may be the least of our worries.

APPENDIX:
A CLASSIC COPES
WITH CRUCIFIXION

IF the Jewish reader of the Hebrew Bible gets a sense of *déjà vu* on first reading the gospels, the Christian reader of the passion narrative will experience the same sensation on a first reading of *Prometheus Bound*, the Greek tragedy generally attributed to Aeschylus. Given the tantalizing series of near-parallels, the temptation to "compare and contrast" *Prometheus Bound* and passion narrative is irresistible. Indeed, some commentators claim that the Church Fathers saw *Prometheus* as a Christ-figure. By contrast, for the ultra-romantic Shelley, Prometheus exemplified human rebellion against an unjust God.

The main character of the *dramatis personae* presented by Aeschylus, the rebel-hero Prometheus, dominates the stage to the point that he never leaves it throughout the play. The corresponding villain, if that is not too Victorian a term, is the tyrannical Zeus (more specifically and tellingly—The Father), who is offstage throughout. We do not need a Greek chorus to cue us to the fact that all our sympathies will remain with the onstage Prometheus.

at the expense of the absentee Father. Indeed, the tyrannical Father of *Prometheus Bound* stands in such contrast to the just Zeus of the *Oresteia* that most modern scholars question the authenticity of the former, and linguistic and stylistic analysis tend to further erode the traditional attribution.

When the play opens, the Father has already passed sentence on Prometheus, ordering that he be *nailed* to a rock. This sentence is to be executed not just outside the city walls, but at the very edge of the inhabited world, a pathless wilderness.

Prometheus Bound serves to emphasize that mockery of the crucified is an essential component of crucifixion, and not just an incidental by-product. When Prometheus (Forethought) has been bound to the rock and the last nail driven in, the malevolent demon Might berates him:

> Now, play the insolent; now, plunder the gods' privileges and give them to creatures of a day....What drop of our sufferings can mortals spare you? The gods named you wrongly when they called you Forethought; you need Forethought to extricate yourself from this contrivance.

For Prometheus, this exposure to mockery is the cruelest of his punishments:

> Would that he had hurled me
> underneath the earth and underneath
> the House of Hades, host to the dead—yes,
> down to limitless Tartarus,
> yes, though he bound me cruelly in chains unbreakable,
> so neither God nor any other being might have found joy in gloating over me. Now I hang, the plaything of the winds, my enemies can laugh at what I suffer.

Of what *hamartia* (generally translated *sin*; etymologically "missing the mark") was Prometheus guilty? He put his overweening *philanthropia* (love of humankind) above the deference demanded by The Father. This we learn from Hephaestus, the smith, as he reluctantly hammers in the nails—just obeying orders in fear of a Father impervious to prayer:

> Such is the reward you reap of your man-loving disposition, for you, a god, feared not the anger of the gods, but gave honors to mortals beyond what was just. Wherefore you shall mount guard on this unlovely rock, upright, sleepless, not bending the knee. Many a groan and many a lamentation you shall utter, but they shall not serve you. For the mind of Zeus is hard to soften with prayer and every ruler is harsh whose rule is new.

The final reference to a new regime reflects the recent over-throw of Cronus, king of heaven, by his son Zeus. While this led to the usual conferring of privileges on the usurper's supporters among the gods, a different fate was planned for mere humans, as Prometheus explains:

> ...but to the unhappy breed of mankind he gave no heed, intending to blot the race out and create a new. Against these plans none stood save I: I dared. I rescued men from shattering destruction that would have carried them to Hades' house; and therefore I am tortured on this rock, a bitterness to suffer, and a pain to pitiful eyes. I gave to mortal man a precedence over myself in pity: I can win no pity: pitiless is he that thus chastises me, a spectacle bringing dishonor on the name of Zeus.

This project of Zeus to wipe out existing humankind and start afresh with new people echoes ancient Babylonian myths adapted into the biblical story of the flood. The Torah continues with other stories of the intervention of the compassionate intercessor warding off the Lord's destroying anger. Abraham bargains, driving down the number of worthy ones needed to avert the general destruction. Moses, in a particularly poignant passage (considering the way his people have treated him), elects solidarity with his sinful people over a higher destiny if that should be the ultimate choice:

So Moses went back to the LORD and said, "Oh, what a great sin these people have committed! They have made themselves gods of gold. But now, please forgive their sin—but if not, then blot me out of the book you have written" (Ex 32:31–32).

Paul echoes this sentiment in his letter to the Romans:

I speak the truth in Christ—I am not lying, my conscience confirms it in the Holy Spirit—I have great sorrow and unceasing anguish in my heart. For I could wish that I myself were cursed and cut off from Christ for the sake of my brothers, those of my own race, the people of Israel. (Rom 9:1–4).

In the fourth gospel Jesus is the *philanthropos* par excellence: "Having loved his own who were in the world, he loved them to the end" (13:1). "Greater love has no one than this, that he lay down his life for his friends" (15:13).

A vast difference between the crucifixion of Jesus and that of Prometheus lies in the role of the Father.

Just as Moses lifted up the snake in the desert, so the Son of Man must be lifted up, that everyone who believes in him may have eternal life. For God so loved the world that he gave his one and only Son, that whoever believes in him shall not perish but have eternal life. (Jn 3:14–16)

Thus, the *philanthropia* of Jesus has its ultimate origin in the *philanthropia* of the Father. (How this could possibly be expressed through the crucifixion of Jesus was the problem the early Christians wrestled with, as traced in the main part of our essay—*The Trauma of the Cross*.) The Father in *Prometheus Bound* is closer to the paranoid Herods depicted by Matthew and Josephus.[1] This can go far to explain the fact that when Greek patristic literature is scoured for texts comparing the crucified Jesus to Aeschylus, we find scant pickings, amounting to little more than cameo appearances of Prometheus in Tatian and Clement of Alexandria.

In his *Oratio ad Graecos* Tatian, after a passing reference to the Greek myth of Prometheus as "creator of humankind," returns in a later passage with a further sampling of Greek myths, including, "Prometheus, chained to the Caucasus, endured punishment for his benefaction to men. According to you Zeus is jealous and hid the dream because he wanted mankind to be destroyed." Thus, the figure that Zeus cuts destroys any temptation to explore a Caucasus/ Golgotha parallel. Tatian was in this polemical work heaping scorn on the more fantastic elements of Greek mythology. Moreover, in the same work Tatian turns his mockery of Greek claims to culture on the earthier productions of their beloved theater:

> *I refuse to stand and gape at a chanting crowd, and I do not want to ape the antics of someone gesticulating and writhing in an unnatural way. Is there any kind of spectacle left for you to devise? They blow their noses and use foul language, they posture obscenely and demonstrate on the stage how to commit adultery in full view of your daughters and boys.*

Clearly a man with such a negative attitude to the theater, and such was common among early Christian writers, was not going to draw parallels between *Prometheus Bound* and the passion narrative.

In his *Stromata* Clement of Alexandria is somewhat less hostile to Hellenistic culture, conceding with a touch of condescension that:

> *There is in philosophy, which was stolen as if by a Prometheus, a spark of fire which can give light if we feed it properly; it is a trace of wisdom, inciting one to turn to God. That is how the Greek philosophers can be called "thieves and robbers," because before the advent of the Lord they took from the Hebrew prophets bits of the truth, without reaching true knowledge, appropriating them as their own thoughts.*

Other references to Prometheus in the *Stromata* are equally tangential.

A search of other early Christian products of classic education—Tertullian, Lactantius, Justin, Origen, Augustine—fails to uncover a single text comparing *Prometheus Bound* and the passion narrative. Paleo-Christian art, lavish in representations of an Orpheus/Jesus, balks at a Prometheus/Jesus.

Just as the four evangelists drew upon the Hebrew scriptures to fashion their passion narratives, Aeschylus looked to earlier Greek models. While he characterizes the bulk of his writings as "morsels from the banquet of Homer," for *Prometheus Bound* he looked to two works by Hesiod: *Works and Days* and *Theogony*. At each stage of his literary evolution, the main character becomes more complex. Prometheus starts out in early Greek folklore as a generic trickster hero, plays a newly serious role in Hesiod and becomes the archetypal rebel in Aeschylus. Similarly, the generic persecuted just one of certain psalms becomes the Suffering Servant of Isaiah, with the main role in the passion of Jeremiah, to culminate in the crucified Jesus.

A play as rich as *Prometheus Bound* deserves more extended analysis. Care should be exercised by all reading *Prometheus Bound* with Christian spectacles, as it has not always been exercised by those reading the gospels with Hellenic spectacles. While Luke may record Jesus as saying, "I have come to bring fire on the earth," it is surely pushing it to see here a flicker of Promethean flame! Hopefully, however, this brief survey of *Prometheus Bound* will serve to highlight the uniqueness of the proto-Christian coping with crucifixion.

This uniqueness is underlined within the New Testament in a famous passage (Acts 17) where the "Apostle to the Gentiles," chased out of the synagogues of Thessalonika and Beroea by hostile Jews (whose colleagues had "received the word with all eagerness, *examining the scriptures daily* to see if these things were so"), is taken to Athens. He continues his preaching in the local synagogue, but also brings his message to the Agora—the market square—thus competing with the "Epicurean and Stoic philosophers" hawking their respective

Ways. He attracts sufficient attention there to warrant his introduction to the more select audience on the *Areopagus*, "who...spent their time in nothing except telling or hearing something new." This is his big chance!

Paul takes his cue from the inscription on a nearby altar: *agnosto theo* (to the unknown god). This, he explains, is the creator God who made heaven and earth, and is not confined to shrines. He made all races so that they should seek him.

The rabbinical Paul now "searches the (Hellenistic) scriptures" for proof-texts. The harvest is meager enough—two quotations. "In him we live and move and have our being," from the Cretan poet Epimenides (c. 600 B.C.) in his *Cretica*, and "We are his offspring," from the Cilician poet Aratus (c. 315–240) in his *Phaenomena*, as well as from Cleanthes (331–233) in his *Hymn to Zeus*.[2]

God could not therefore be a lifeless statue. He overlooks such ignorance, but now calls all to repent, having appointed a judge for all the world, and confirming his authority by raising him from the dead.

The lacunae of this approach are exposed when we compare it with the standard sermons of Peter and Paul throughout Acts. The Hebrew scriptures, a closed book to the typical habitué of the Areopagus, are necessarily jettisoned. But the Hellenistic scriptures yield no comparable depths. They furnish a rudimentary theology, but do little for a christology.

Most significantly, while the sermon ends with a reference to the resurrection of Jesus, there is no mention whatsoever of the manner of his death. Coming from Paul of all people, a catechesis without the cross seems a total aberration.

While some of his listeners "joined him and believed," in general this approach seems to have fallen flat. Paul wastes no more time in Athens, but leaves for Corinth. He never returns to Athens. We have no Epistle to the Athenians. His Areopagus sermon never reappears elsewhere. With all due respect for the riches of Hellenistic culture, the essential Christian message of the cross ("foolishness to the Greeks") makes no sense outside the matrix of the Hebrew Scriptures.

NOTES

CHAPTER 1

1. Abraham Lincoln, Gettysburg Address.

2. *The Orthodox Corruption of Scripture: The Effect of Early Christological Controversies on the Text of the New Testament.* New York: Oxford University Press, 1993.

3. Ernst Käsemann purports to identify a telltale "strand of naïve docetism" in the passion narrative which he sees as a "mere postscript" to the fourth gospel. For a review of the resultant debate see Gerard A. Sloyan: *What are They Saying about John?* (Mahwah, N.J.: Paulist Press, 1991), 58–59.

4. A similar assertion surfaces in a fourteenth-century manual for inquisitors, in a chapter devoted to "The Errors of the Beguines":

> ...that Christ was alive while he was hanging on the cross after the lance had pierced his side, saying that the soul of Christ still resided in his body. Since Christ was totally exhausted, to the onlookers he appeared to be dead. Therefore John in his gospel said that he was then dead because he seemed dead [*quia mortuus apparebat*]; but Matthew in his gospel wrote that Christ was alive, for so it truly was. But the Church erased this from Matthew's gospel lest it should appear to contradict John's gospel. (Bernard Gui: *Manuel*

de l'Inquisiteur, vol. 1, p. 138. *Les Classiques de l'Histoire de France au Moyen Âge.* G. Mollat, ed. and trans. 2 vols. Paris: Société d'Édition "Les Belles Lettres," 1926.)

5. The word "neo-Gnostic" lingers on as a pejorative label in contemporary religious polemics.

CHAPTER 2

1. Psalm 137:5.
2. "Although Jewish history is replete with disaster, none has been so radical in its total impact as the Holocaust" (Richard L. Rubenstein: *After Auschwitz*, p. X.). How, then, does the contemporary Jew cope with the Holocaust? "...[F]or a generation there generally was theological silence, until 1966, when Richard Rubenstein's book, *After Auschwitz*, announced that the post-Holocaust theological age had begun" (Jerome Eckstein: "The Holocaust and Jewish Theology" in *In the Aftermath of the Holocaust*, Jacob Neusner, ed. [New York: Garland, 1993). More recently a longer and suggestive perspective is suggested by Rubenstein himself: "It is sometimes said that Holocaust theology was born in the nineteen sixties when, after a generation of silence, theologians finally turned to the extermination of Europe's Jews and began to seek for religious meaning in the most devastating catastrophe that befell the Jewish people since the fall of Jerusalem" ("The Fall of Jerusalem and the Birth of Holocaust Theology" in Jacob Neusner, ed., *Judaism Transcends Catastrophe: God, Torah, and Israel Beyond the Holocaust*, Vol. I, *Faith Renewed*, Macon, Ga.: Mercer University Press, 1994). Obviously the generation of the Holocaust was a generation in a protracted state of shock, which initially said more than it wrote. Only the passage of time would trigger writings and restore perspective.
3. Ancient Israel mirrors a belief held by its Middle Eastern neighbors: the destruction of city and temple is traceable to the inhabitants' neglect of that city's deity.
4. The "remodeling" took 70 years to complete. For the broader context, see Duane W. Roller: *The Building Program of Herod the Great* (University of California Press, 1998).

5. The Northern Irish reader of Josephus will not fail to note that the Jewish freedom fighters were split into innumerable factions, often warring among themselves, with individual leaders feathering their financial nests, and meting out summary justice to those who counseled a negotiated settlement with Rome. Within the Holy Land, communities of Jews lived side by side with communities of Hellenized Syrians, and mutual bouts of ethnic cleansing were endemic. The use of Syrian auxiliaries by Rome's army of occupation would suggest a model for recent British use of Scottish regiments in Northern Ireland, consistent with British use of Irish regiments to put down Scottish rebellion in the eighteenth century.

6. Jesus asked him, "What is your name?" "Legion," he said, because many devils had entered him (Lk 8:30).

7. Service for *Tish'a be-Av*—a fast day still observed on the ninth of Av by Orthodox Jews in memory of the destruction of the first and second temples. On this day the study of Torah is forbidden "because it is a source of joy," with the following significant exceptions: Lamentations of Jeremiah, Job, the curses in Leviticus (26:14–42), portions of Jeremiah.

CHAPTER 3

1. Deuteronomy 21:23.

2. J. B. Green, "Crucifixion." In *Dictionary of Jesus and the Gospels* (Downers Grove, Ill.: Intervarsity Press, 1992).

3. Ibid.

4. Ep. 1.16.46–48.

5. Rab. Perd. 16.

6. *Contra Celsum*, 6:34. A modern Celsus might ask: If Jesus had been executed in the electric chair, would our bishops sport gold electric chairs on their chests?

7. H. Leclerq, "Croix et Crucifix." In III *Dictionnaire d'Archéologie Chrétienne de de Liturgie* (Paris: Letouzey et Ane, 1914), 3046, 3052.

8. M. Nardelli, *La Chiesa di Roma nel I Secolo* (Brescia: Franciscanum, 1967), 150.

9. Byron R. McCabe, "'Where No One Had Yet Been Laid.' The Shame of Jesus' Burial." In *Society of Biblical Literature*, 1993, Seminar Papers (Atlanta: n.d.), 473–84.

10. Semahot 8.1. The custom of rapid burial, with its awareness of the attendant danger of premature burial, adds an intriguing footnote to the gospel story of the resurrection of the daughter of the ruler of the synagogue ("The child is not dead, but sleeping" [Mk 5:39]).

11. M. Sanh. 6:5.

CHAPTER 4

1. Gary Taylor, *Cultural Selection* (New York: Basic Books, 1996).

2. Compare our footnote 1 above, with its conclusion: "Obviously the generation of the Holocaust was a generation in a protracted state of shock, which initially said more than it wrote. Only the passage of time would trigger writings and restore perspective."

3. Joseph A. Fitzmyer, *The Gospel according to Luke*, Anchor Bible, volume 28A (New York: Doubleday, 1985), 1558.

CHAPTER 5

1. Isaiah 53:3.

2. U. P. McCaffrey, *Psalm Quotations in the Passion Narratives of the Gospels in 14 Neotestamentica* (Bloemfontein, 1981), 74.

3. Ibid., 73.

4. Centuries later Muslims would reinterpret this story. The tradition that "Ibrahim" chose "Ishaq" (Isaac, the father of Israel) for sacrifice is rejected by the Qur'an. It was really Ishmael, the father of the Arabs, and the event is commemorated in the great pilgrimage to Mecca. Thus do the three "Peoples of the Book" interpret the same book differently.

5. Two other extra-canonical versions of the death of Judas are traced to the second-century writer Papias. After a painstaking review of all four accounts and sundry attempts, ancient and modern, to "reconcile" them, Raymond Brown concludes: "The common antecedent of the four accounts, then, is not one form of death but the sudden violence of the death that needed interpretation by the Scriptures" (*The Death of the Messiah*, p. 1410.)

6. The ongoing availability of such passages for reapplication is illustrated by Eric van Tassell in *The Purcell Companion*.

94   THE TRAUMA OF THE CROSS

Purcell composed music for the King's chapel, "And politics probably underlay, far more often than we can now prove, the selection or editing of anthem texts for ordinary or special Chapel Royal services, to support the official line on the issues of the day—implicitly identifying the much-plotted-against Charles II with the embattled King David of the Psalms, or even reading Isaiah's 'Suffering Servant' as an antetype of the martyred Charles I." (p. 102). Here we see how the "suffering" texts from the psalms and Isaiah can be liturgically applied so that a later, Christian king is perceived as a Christ-figure.

7. "Isaiah" in David Rosenberg, ed., *Congregation: Contemporary Writers Read the Jewish Bible* (New York: Harcourt Brace Jovanovich, 1987), 145.

8. "Isaiah" in Robert Alter/Frank Kermode, eds., *The Literary Guide to the Bible* (Cambridge: Belknap Press, 1987), 166.

CHAPTER 6

1. Jeremiah 20:7.

2. An important function of the temple police is defined in Jeremiah 29:26: "The Lord himself has made you priest instead of the priest Jehoiada, so that there may be officers in the house of the Lord *to control any madman who plays the prophet*, to put him in the stocks and the collar." Since prisoners put on public display in the stocks were liable to have passers-by throw stones at them, such punishment could be lethal. The fourth gospel has eight references to the temple police; Luke has two.

3. According to George Fox (*Journal*, I, 38) the name "Quaker" was first given to himself and his followers by Justice Bennet at Derby in 1650, "because I bid them tremble at the Word of the Lord." The *Oxford English Dictionary* notes, "The name has never been adopted by the Friends themselves, but is not now regarded as a term of reproach." The Dictionary cites a 1651 work saying: "We have many Sects now abroad: Ranters, Seekers, Shakers, Quakers, and now Creepers."

4. Recorded by the *Oxford English Dictionary* as "U.S. Slang." All the literary examples given are post-1920, and include John Dos Passos, Henry Miller and Ezra Pound.

5. *Auctor nominis eius Christus Tiberio imperitante per procuratorem Pontium Pilatum supplicio adfectus erat.* Tacitus: *Annales* XV, 44.

CHAPTER 7

1. Psalm 22:7

2. It has been claimed that the trio Law/Prophets/Psalms embraces the whole of the Hebrew scriptures, so that the "Psalms" include all those books not included in the first two categories—books included in an alternative formulation under the generic name of "Writings" (Kethubim). In this chapter we will, however, focus on the Psalter.

3. The opening chapter of Umberto Eco's *The Name of the Rose* brings home a vital distinction for the modern reader: When moderns want to know what a horse looks like, they head out to the paddock to observe one; when medieval people want to know what a horse looks like, they head to the library to consult the standard authority on horses (Isidore of Seville). Similarly, the crucifixion was best understood, not by the observers on Calvary, but by the readers of the authoritative texts.

4. The death of a king would have been a potential occasion for discontented vassals to throw off the royal yoke. Psalm 2 was originally a coronation ode, asserting the divine origin of the successor king's appointment, and warning his more powerful subjects to toe the line. The anointing with oil (by the high priest) put the divine seal on the new king, the Lord's own Anointed, the Messiah (Hebrew) or *Christos* (Greek). The El Amarna correspondence shows Psalm 2 to be a standard Syro-Palestinian scenario with stock characters. For a vestigial modern application, see Elizabeth II, *by the grace of God* Queen of England, Scotland, Wales and Northern Ireland...

CHAPTER 8

1. Such attributions "stem from the late second century, and represent an educated guess of authorship by church scholars of that period who were putting together traditions and guesses pertinent to attribution. To this a caution must be added: The ancient concept of authorship was often less rigorous than our own, at times amounting to identifying only the authority behind a work (however distant), rather than the writer." Brown: *Death*, I, 4, footnote 2.

2. The following discussion draws on A. G. Martimort: *Église en Priére: Introduction à la Liturgie* (Tournai: Desclée de Brouwer, 1965).

3. The fourth gospel, here as elsewhere, rewrites the script to conform to its own theology. Jesus on his cross is already "lifted up" into glory. There is no darkness over the cross.

4. And so to work. The first day of the week was an ordinary workday, until Constantine changed that too. So the weekly gathering of the faithful was inserted into the night between the Jewish Sabbath day of rest, the seventh day, which ended Saturday evening, and the first day (sometimes called, in Janus fashion, the eighth day).

5. A point still being made in 1799 by the acknowledged "father of nineteenth century theology," Friedrich Schleiermacher, in his first published work under the significant title: *On Religion: Speeches to its Cultured Despisers*. The salons of the eighteenth century "Enlightenment" had seen a resurgence of the disdain that was prevalent in Roman society until Constantine.

CHAPTER 9

1. 1 Corinthians 1:23.

2. The Lucan search the scriptures imperative resonates in Luke's report of Paul's maiden sabbath sermon at Antioch in Pisidia: The people and leaders of Jerusalem had not recognized Jesus, "or understood *the words of the prophets* that are read every sabbath. *They fulfilled those words* by condemning him...When *they had carried out everything that was written about him* they took him down from the tree and laid him in the tomb (Acts 13, with echoes of Ps 2, Is 55, Ps 16, Hab 1).

CHAPTER 10

1. Modern Anzio, just south of Rome on the coast, was the site of a disastrous Allied landing in World War II, as evidenced by a huge military cemetery.

2. Interesting, in the context of the present essay, that Nero should "search the (Roman) scriptures" for answers to the question: why have the gods done this to the city? In Greco-Roman culture, the epic poems of Homer were virtually Holy Writ. In his *Iliad* Homer sings of the fiery destruction of Troy (Ilium). It is suggested that the actual text sung by Nero may have been that of Juvenal's derivative *Troica*.

3. "...Nero, publicly announcing himself as the chief enemy of God, was led on in his fury to slaughter the apostles. Paul is therefore said to have been beheaded at Rome, and Peter to have been crucified under him. And this account is confirmed by the fact that the names of Peter and Paul still remain in the cemeteries of that city even to this day" (Eusebius: *Ecclesiastical History*, XXV). Tradition has it that Peter was crucified hanging upside-down. This is not improbable, given that Josephus reports that during the siege of Jerusalem the Romans scourged their prisoners and crucified them opposite the city walls, "The soldiers out of rage and hatred amused themselves by nailing their prisoners in different positions" (*Jewish Wars*, 5.11.1).

4. "The earliest explicit statement about Mark as the author of a Gospel came from Papias of Hierapolis (early 2d cent., quoted in Eusebius, HE 3.39.15): 'Mark, having become Peter's interpreter, wrote down accurately whatever he remembered of what was said or done by the Lord, however not in order.' On the strength of Papias's statement and the affirmation of it by other early Christian writers, the Gospel is traditionally ascribed to Mark "the interpreter of Peter" and placed in Rome after Peter's death ca. A.D. 64–67" (Daniel J. Harrington, S.J.: "The Gospel according to Mark" in *The New Jerome Biblical Commentary*, Brown/Fitzmyer/Murphy, eds. [Englewood Cliffs, N.J.: Prentice-Hall, 1990]). Presumably the fisherman from Galilee preaching in Rome would indeed need an interpreter (at that time Greek rather than Latin), who would later be the logical literary executor on Peter's death.

5. *Times Literary Supplement* (4/14/95), 26.

6. This ghoulish tradition was to be observed on a grand scale during the Holocaust.

7. In Greek tragedy this is also the theme of *Antigone* (written by Sophocles and first performed c. 442 B.C.), the loyal sister who laments:

> But the unhappy corpse of Polyneices
> he [Creon] has proclaimed to all the citizens,
> they say, no man may hide
> in a grave nor mourn in funeral
> but leave unwept, unburied, a dainty treasure
> for the birds that see him, for their feast's delight.

Creon:

> *You shall leave him without burial; you shall watch him*
> *chewed up by birds and dogs and violated.*

The Greeks apparently believed that the dead person's ghost could not enter Hades until

the body had been covered. See Aeschylus: *Seven against Thebes*, ll. 1006–1015. Indeed, the very first sentence of Homer's *Iliad* is a lament for the "many valiant souls of warriors [who] made themselves to be a spoil for dogs and all manner of birds."

8. *La Chiesa di Roma nel I Secolo* (Brescia: Franciscanum, 1967), 150.
9. "The Acts of Peter" in Willis Barnstone, ed., *The Other Bible* (San Francisco: Harper & Row, 1984), 442.
10. Ibid., 442–43.
11. Ibid., 443.
12. M. Nardelli, *La Chiesa di Roma nel I Secolo*, 151.
13. Frank J. Matera, *Passion Narratives and Gospel Theologies* (Mahwah, N.J.: Paulist Press, 1986), 221.

CHAPTER 11

1. John 2:19.
2. Whether the *Book of Signs* had its autonomous publication history before its appearance in the first half of the fourth gospel is a matter of debate among scholars. Our focus is on the Johannine "edition."
3. The extent to which the second temple had become a bank is already apparent in 2 Maccabees 3, where c. 187 B.C. King Seleucus sends his minister to seize temple funds: "...the high priest declared that [these funds] consisted partly of deposits of widows and orphans and partly of deposits of Hyrcanus the Tobiad, a man of very high position...The depositors had put their trust in the sanctity of the place and in the dignity and inviolability of the temple venerated throughout the whole world...The priests...prayed heavenward to the Establisher of the laws of deposits to keep them safe for the depositors."

4. A German psychiatrist's early (1905) attempt to psychoanalyze Jesus saw in this incident proof that Jesus was mentally unstable.

5. "John" labels the water-into-wine and the curing of the royal official's son (both performed at Cana) as the first and second signs. The temple incident is sandwiched between these two signs. This did not prevent Alfred Loisy in the *Origins of the New Testament* from writing "The second sign worked by Jesus is the expulsion of the traders from the Temple (2:13–17)." This episode is not included in the hypothetical Signs Gospel as reconstructed by Fortna and others. C. H. Dodd, however, suggests that the evangelist considered actions such as the cleansing of the temple as signs. Brown agrees that "It is possible that he did; the Jews did not however" (*The Gospel according to John*, p. 529).

6. A reference to Herod's ambitious remodeling of the second temple, not finally completed until A.D. 64. Since it had begun in 20 B.C., the year of the event recorded here is A.D. 26.

7. See the nuanced assent of Raymond E. Brown, citing Wayne Meeks, E. D. Dodd and J. D. Purvis in *The Community of the Beloved Disciple: The Life, Loves, and Hates of an Individual Church in New Testament Times* (New York: Paulist Press, 1979).

CHAPTER 12

1. John 9:22.

2. *The Community Rule*, 1QS VIII.

3. Kephart/Zellner: *Extraordinary Groups: An Examination of Unconventional Life-Styles* (New York: St. Martin's Press, 1994), p. 27.

4. Given this prevailing anti-synagogue polemic of the fourth gospel, note the convention of medieval crucifixion art recorded by Aquinas: "Beside the cross of Christ the Blessed Virgin is shown on the right side, pointing to the church, and on the left side is John, condemning the synagogue" (In *Opusculo*, 58, c° 31).

5. This has been recently explored at length and with passion by Dominic Crossan: *Who Killed Jesus?: Exposing the Roots of Anti-Semitism in the Gospel Story of the Death of Jesus* (San Francisco: HarperSan Francisco, 1995).

CHAPTER 13

1. This scenario shows how naive it is to imagine pre-Constantinian Christianity as a lost state of primeval innocence, which we now despair to reconstruct.

2. The first page of the *Cambridge Medieval History* poses the fundamental question: where to draw the line between ancient and medieval history? After reviewing various possibilities (including the destruction of Jerusalem), the editors opt for beginning with Constantine. These two competing epochs constitute the bookends of the present study.

3. *Vita Constantini*, 14.

4. In some respects, Constantine may have resembled man-of-the-world Rex in *Brideshead Revisited*, dispatched by his devout future mother-in-law to the Jesuits in London's Farm Street for instruction in the faith. Some days later a bemused Fr. Mowbray reports: "I gave him the catechism to take away. Yesterday I asked him whether Our Lord had more than one nature. He said: 'Just as many as you say, Father.'"

5. *Octavius* XXIX, 6.

6. Ep. IV, 61 = Migne PG LXXIX, 577ff.

7. *De Abraham* II, 7: Migne PL XIV, 498.

CHAPTER 14

1. Seamus Heaney, "The Tollund Man."

2. Gerhard Barth, *Der Tod Jesu Christi im Verständnis des Neuen Testaments*, (Neukirchen-Vluyn: Neukirchner Verlag, 1992).

3. Malcolm W. Browne, *New York Times Review of Books* (8/27/95).

4. "Already [Volume 1] introduced the theory that the [Passion Narrative] arose not from the memory of what happened but simply from imaginative reflection on the [Old Testament], especially on passages describing the suffering of the just one at the hands of enemies who plot against him, mocking his trust in God. Although I offered reasons for rejecting such a radical approach (at least in regard to the main outline of the canonical Passion Narratives), it is impossible to deny that the Old Testament background influenced heavily early Christian presentation of the passion, highlighting what should be recounted in order to expand the preaching outline into dramatic narratives. Moreover, in passion material which did not go through the cru-

cible of common knowledge or synagogue debate and in which popular imagination was allowed freer rein...Old Testament influence was truly creative" (*The Death of the Messiah*, vol. 2, p. 1445).

APPENDIX

1. Our *Prometheus Bound* is the only intact survivor of a trilogy, and commentators are tempted to imagine a final reconciliation between the two main protagonists.

2. Paul quotes Greek poets elsewhere as well, but to even more generic effect. (1 Cor 15:33: "Bad company corrupts good character" from the Greek comedy *Thais* (by Menander); Titus 1:12: "Even one of their own prophets has said, 'Cretans are always liars, evil brutes, lazy gluttons'" (Epimenides, a sixth-century B.C. native of Knossos, Crete). Note, poet equals prophet.

WORKS CONSULTED

THIS list has no pretentions to completeness, and is merely for the convenience of the reader who may wish to pursue a point further.

PRIMARY SOURCES

Aeschylus. *Prometheus Bound.* David Grene and Richard Lattimore, eds. Chicago and London: University of Chicago Press, 1991.

Barnstone, Willis, ed. *The Other Bible.* San Francisco: Harper & Row, 1984.

Cicero. *The Speeches.* Loeb Classical Library, 1952.

Gui, Bernard. *Manuel de l'"Inquisiteur.* Les Classiques de l'Histoire de France au Moyens Âge. G. Mollat, trans. and ed. 2 vols. Paris: Société d'Édition "Les Belles Lettres," 1926.

Josephus. *The Jewish Wars.* William Whiston, trans. and ed. Peabody Mass.: Hendrickson Publishers, 1988.

Tacitus. *The Annals.* Loeb Classsical Library, 1937.

Tatian: *Oratio ad Graecos.* Oxford: Clarendon Press, 1982.

SECONDARY WORKS

Barret, C. K. "The House of Prayer and the Den of Thieves." In *Jesus and Paulus. Festschrift für Werner Georg Kummel zum 70 Geburtstag.* E. Earle Ellis and Erich Grasser, eds. Gottingen: Vandenhoek and Ruprecht, 1975.

Barth, Gerhard. *Der Tod Jesu Christi im Verständnis des Neuen Testaments.* Neukirchen-Vluyn: Neukirchener Verlag, 1992.

Binz, Stephen J. *The Passion and Resurrection Narratives of Jesus. A Commentary.* Collegeville, Minn.: Liturgical Press, 1989.

Brown, Raymond E. *The Death of the Messiah. A Commentary on the Passion Narratives in the Four Gospels.* 2 vols. New York: Doubleday, 1994.

————. *The Gospel according to John.* New York: Doubleday, 1996-1970.

————. *The Community of The Beloved Disciple: The Life, Loves, and Hates of an Individual Church in New Testament Times.* New York: Paulist Press, 1979.

Brown, Raymond E., Joseph A. Fitzmyer, and Roland E. Murphy, eds. *The New Jerome Biblical Commentary.* Englewood Cliffs, N.J.: Prentice-Hall, 1990.

Cohn, H. H. "Crucifixion." In 5 *Encyclopedia Judaica* 1134. Jerusalem: McMillan, 1971. "Cross." In *The Eerdman's Bible Dictionary* 246. Grand Rapids: Eerdmans, 1987.

Crossan, Dominic. *The Cross that Spoke. The Origins of the Passion Narrative.* San Francisco: Harper & Row, 1988.

————. *Who Killed Jesus? Exposing the Roots of Anti-Semitism in the Gospel Story of the Death of Jesus.* San Francisco: HarperSanFrancisco, 1995.

Daniélou, J. "Cross." In I *Sacramentum Verbi: An Encyclopedia of Biblical Theology,* 155. Johannes B. Bauer, ed. New York: Herder and Herder, 1970.

Donahue, J. "From Passion Traditions to Passion Narrative." In *The Passion in Mark: Studies in Mark 14–16,* 1–20. W. Kelber, ed. Philadelphia: Fortress Press, 1976.

de Durand, M. G. "Prométhée dans la Littérature Chrétienne Antique." In *Revue des Études Augustiniennes* 41 (1995): 217–29.

Eckstein, Jerome. "The Holocaust and Jewish Theology." In *In the Aftermath of the Holocaust*. Jacob Neusner, ed. New York: Garland, 1993.

Ehrman, Bart. D. *The Ordhodox Corruption of Scripture*. New York: Oxford University Press, 1993.

Fitzmyer, Joseph A. "Crucifixion in Ancient Palestine, Qumran Literature, and the New Testament." In *Catholic Biblical Quarterly* 40(1978):493–513.

Green, J. B. "Crucifixion." In *Dictionary of Jesus and the Gospels*, 147. Downers Grove, Ill.: Intervarsity Press, 1992.

Haardt, Robert. "Gnosticism." In 2 *Sacramentum Mundi. An Encyclopedia of Theology* 381. New York: Herder and Herder, 1968.

Harrington, Daniel J. "The Gospel according to Mark." In *The New Jerome Biblical Commentary*. Brown/Fitzmyer/Murphy, eds. Englewood Cliffs, N.J.: Prentice-Hall, 1990.

Horbury, W., ed. *Suffering and Martyrdom in the New Testament*. New York: Cambridge University Press, 1981.

Kephart / Zellner. *Extraordinary Groups. An Examination of Unconventional Life-Styles*. New York: St Martin's Press, 1994.

Leclerq, H. "Croix et Crucifix." In III *Dictionnaire d'Archéologie Chrétienne et de Liturgie* 3046. Paris: Letouzey et Ane, 1914.

Loisy, Alfred. *The Origins of the New Testament*. London: George Allen and Unwin, 1950.

Matera, F. *The Kingship of Jesus. Composition and Theology in Mark 15*. Chico, Cal.: Scholars' Press, 1982.

———. *Passion Narratives and Gospel Theologies*. Mahwah, N.J.: Paulist Press, 1986.

McCaffrey, U. P. *Psalm Quotations in the Passion Narratives of the Gospels*. 14 *Neotestamentica. Proceedings of the 16th Meeting of the New Testament Society of South Africa* 74. Bloemfontein: 1981.

McCane, Byron R. "'Where No One Had Yet Been Laid.' The Shame of Jesus' Burial." *In Society of Biblical Literature, 1993 Seminar Papers*. Atlanta: 1994): 473–84.

Nardelli, M. *La Chiesa di Roma nel I Secolo*. Brescia: Franciscanum, 1967.

Neusner, Jacob, ed. *Judaism Transcends Catastrophe. God, Torah, and Israel Beyond the Holocaust*, Vol. I, *Faith Renewed*. Macon, Ga.: Mercer University Press, 1994.

O'Collins, Gerald G. "Crucifixion." In I *The Anchor Bible Dictionary* 1207. New York: Doubleday, 1992.

Pinsky, Robert. "Isaiah." In David Rosenberg, ed. *Congregation. Contemporary Writers Read the Jewish Bible*, 145. New York: Harcourt Brace Jovanovich, 1987.

Rad. J. "Croix." In *Dictionnaire Encyclopédique de la Bible* 316. Brepols: Turnhout (Belgique), 1987.

Rubenstein, Richard L. *After Auschwitz: In the Aftermath of the Holocaust.* Jacob Neusner, ed. New York: Johns Hopkins University Press, 1993.

————."The Fall of Jerusalem and the Birth of Holocaust Theology." In *Judaism Transcends Catastrophe. God, Torah, and Israel Beyond the Holocaust*, Vol. I, *Faith Renewed.* Jacob Neusner, ed. Macon, Ga.: Mercer University Press, 1994.

Schacher, A. A. "Crucifixion (in Art)." In IV *New Catholic Encyclopedia* 486. New York: McGraw-Hill, 1967.

Schneider, J. "σταυρός." In *Theological Dictionary of the New Testament.* Gerhard Friedrich, ed. Grand Rapids: Eerdmans, 1977.

Schökel, Luis Alonso. "Isaiah." In Robert Alter/Frank Kermode, eds. *The Literary Guide to the Bible*, 166. Cambridge: Bellknap Press of the Harvard University Press, 1987.

Senior, Donald. *The Passion of Jesus in the Gospel of Matthew.* Wilmington: Michael Glazier, 1985.

————. *The Passion of Jesus in the Gospel of Mark.* Wilmington: Michael Glazier, 1984.

————. *The Passion of Jesus in the Gospel of Luke.* Wilmington: Michael Glazier, 1989.

————. *The Passion of Jesus in the Gospel of John.* Collegeville, Minn.: Liturgical Press, 1991.

Sepière, M. *L'Image d'un Dieu Souffrant: aux Origines du Crucifix.* Paris: Editions du Cerf, 1994.

Sloyan, Gerard S. *What Are They Saying about John?* Mahwah, N.J.: Paulist Press, 1991.

Zias, Joseph, and Eliezer Sekels. "The Crucified Man from Giv'at ha-Mivtar: A Reappraisal." In *Israeli Exploration Journal* 35 (1995):22–27.